Vermont Exit Ramps II

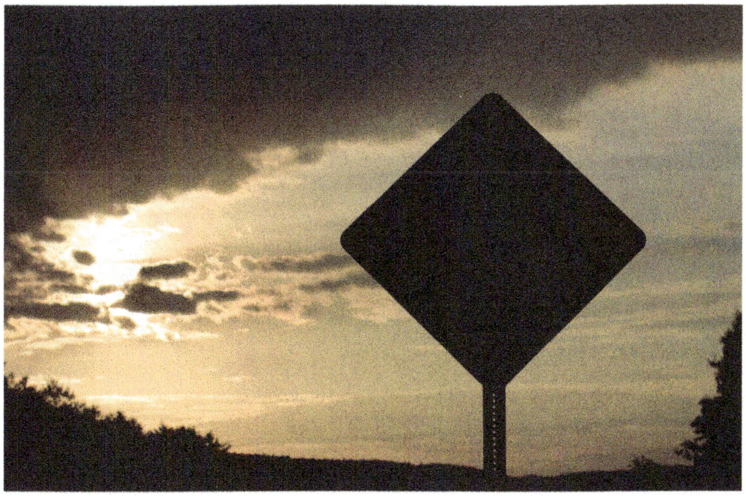

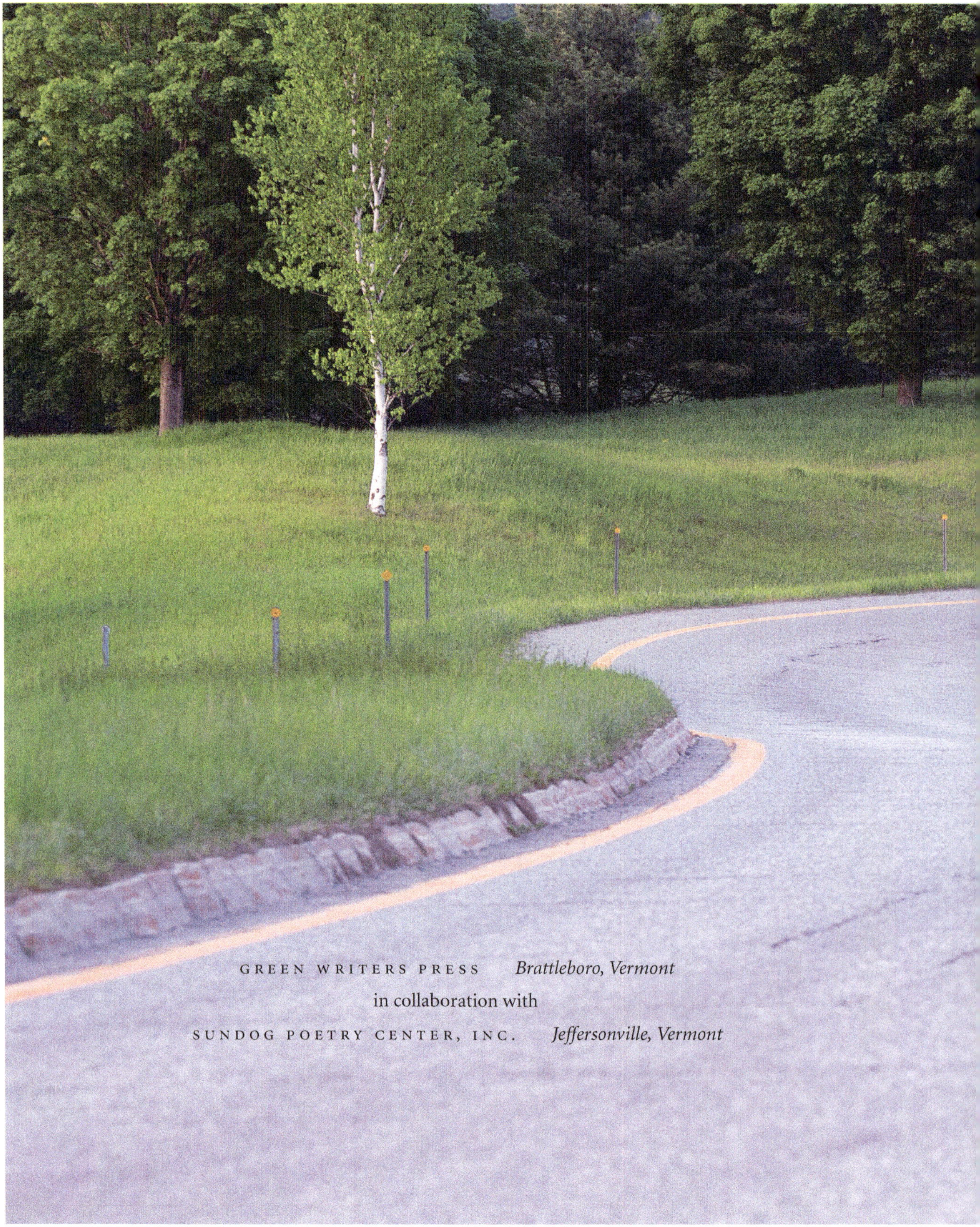

GREEN WRITERS PRESS *Brattleboro, Vermont*
in collaboration with
SUNDOG POETRY CENTER, INC. *Jeffersonville, Vermont*

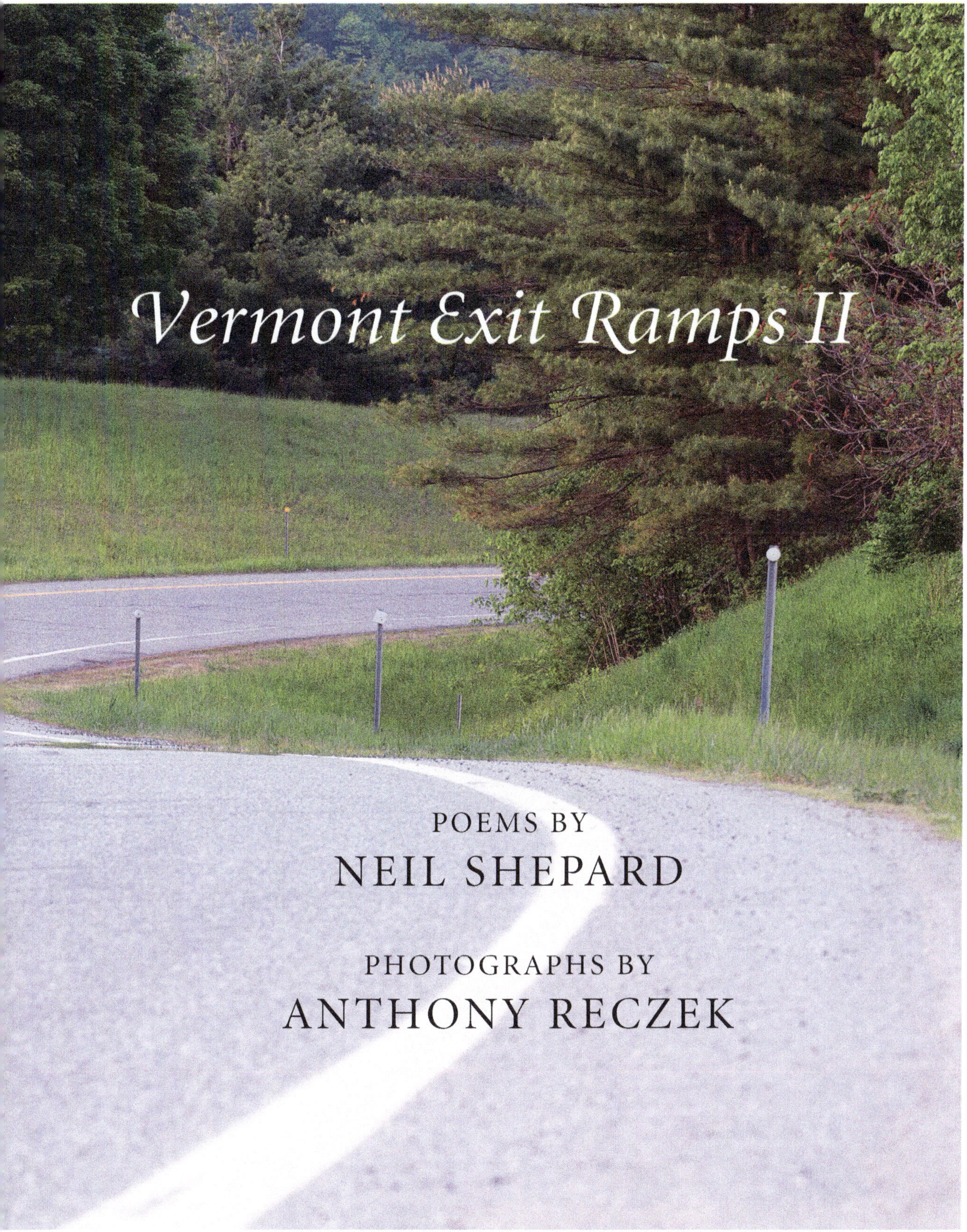

Vermont Exit Ramps II

POEMS BY

NEIL SHEPARD

PHOTOGRAPHS BY

ANTHONY RECZEK

Printed in the United States

10 9 8 7 6 5 4 3 2 1

ISBN: 978-0-9962676-4-9

Green Writers Press is a Vermont-based publisher whose mission is to spread a message of hope and renewal through the words and images we publish. Throughout we will adhere to our commitment to preserving and protecting the natural resources of the earth. To that end, a percentage of our proceeds will be donated to environmental activist groups. Green Writers Press gratefully acknowledges support from our donors, friends, and readers to help support the environment and our publishing initiative.

Giving Voice to Writers & Artists Who Will Make the World a Better Place
Green Writers Press | Brattleboro, Vermont
www.greenwriterspress.com

Published in collaboration with Sundog Poetry Center, Inc.
Jeffersonville, Vermont 05464

As a 501(c)3 charitable organization, it is the mission of Sundog Poetry Center, Inc. to promote poetry as necessary to the enrichment of our cultural lives, support poets in their work and create audiences for their poetry, and provide ways to share poetry throughout the Vermont community. Sundog Poetry Center, Inc. donates 5% of the proceeds from the sale of this book to the Vermont Arts Council.

PRINTED ON PAPER WITH PULP THAT COMES FROM FSC-CERTIFIED FORESTS, MANAGED FORESTS THAT GUARANTEE RESPONSIBLE ENVIRONMENTAL, SOCIAL AND ECONOMIC PRACTICES BY LIGHTNING SOURCE. ALL WOOD PRODUCT COMPONENTS USED IN BLACK & WHITE, STANDARD COLOR, OR SELECT COLOR PAPERBACK BOOKS, UTILIZING EITHER CREAM OR WHITE BOOKBLOCK PAPER THAT ARE MANUFACTURED IN THE LAVERGNE, TENNESSEE PRODUCTION CENTER ARE SUSTAINABLE FORESTRY INITIATIVE® (SFI®) CERTIFIED SOURCING.

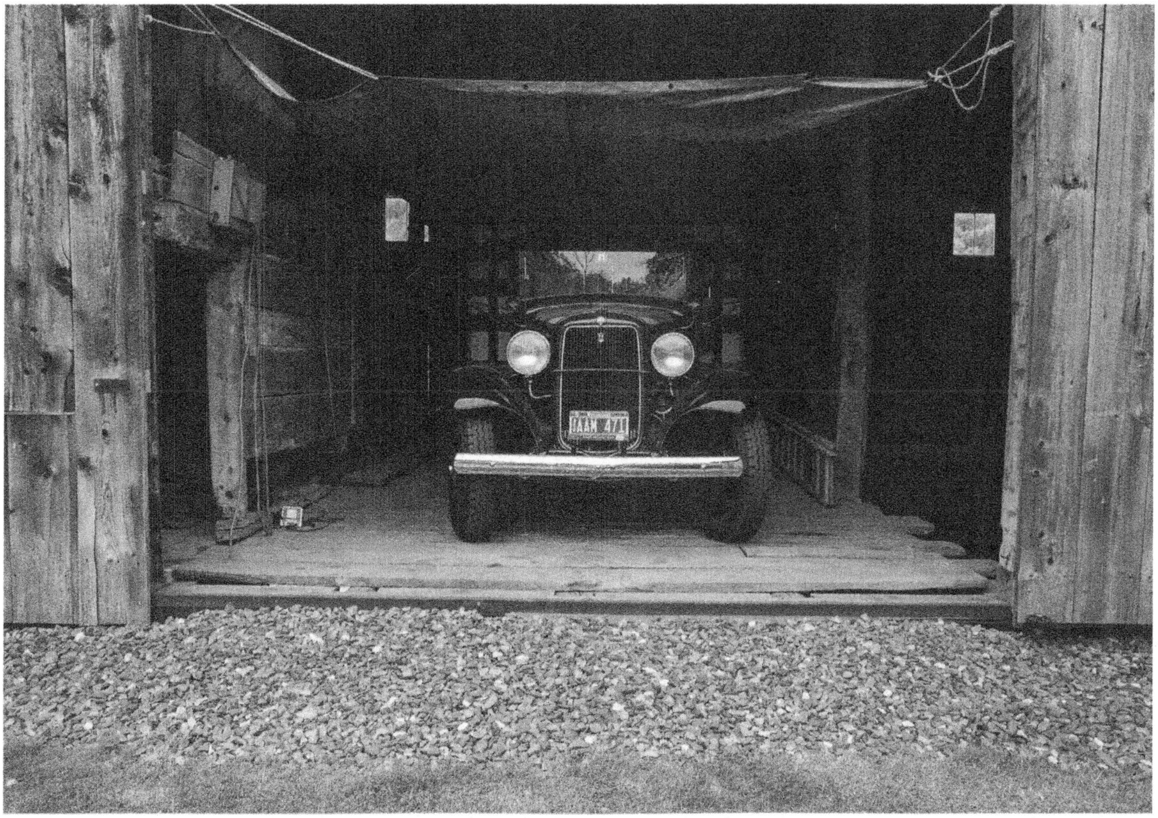

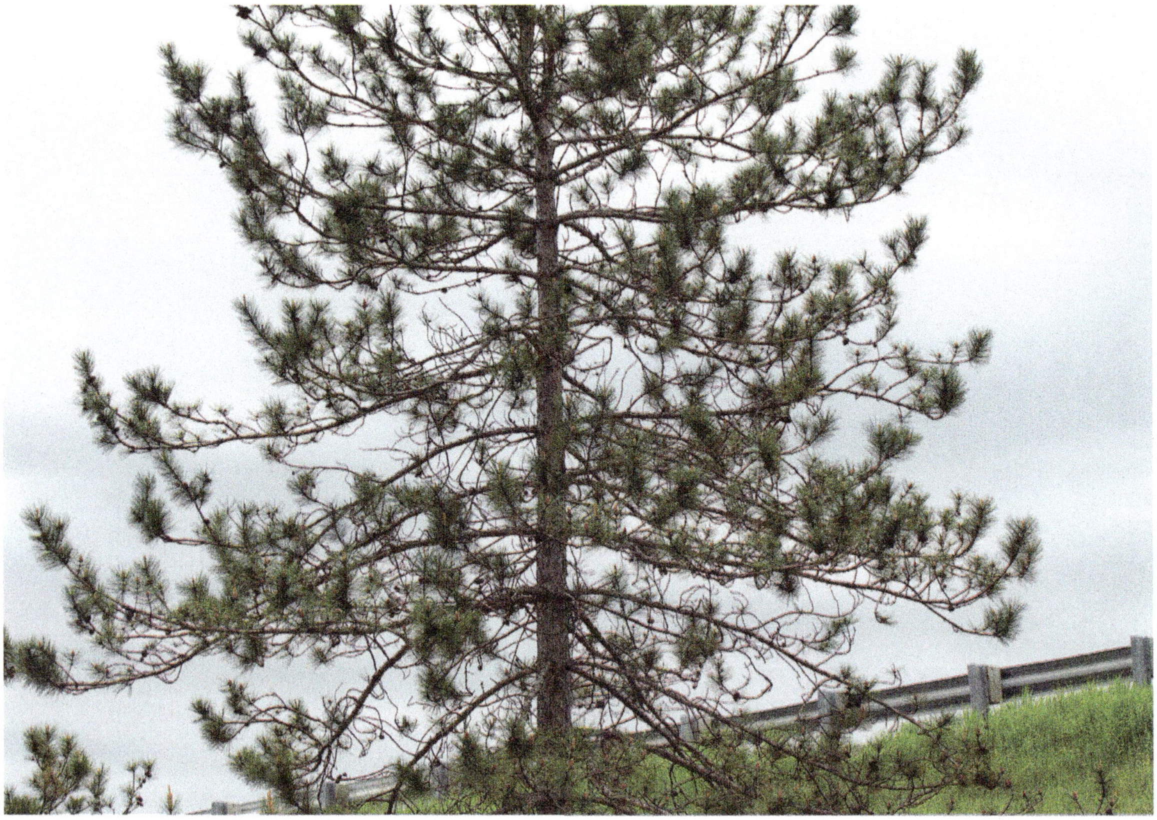

Contents

Introduction

INTRODUCTORY INTERVIEW CONDUCTED BY 8 EXIT RAMPS

Exit 1: What's so compelling about Vermont exit ramps?

PERHAPS IN OTHER PARTS OF AMERICA the exits off highways offer nothing special, but in Vermont many of the exits are beautiful little unclaimed pieces of meadow or woodland that I started calling, generically, ramplands. I'm intrigued by places that have been ravaged and recovered, places that were dynamited, bulldozed, ruined. Then, once the forces of "progress" move elsewhere, these places regenerate and reclaim their little domains of marsh grass, pine grove or granite vista.

Exit 2: What were the specific conditions that generated these poems?

AFTER THE USUAL ATTRITION FROM A YEAR OF TEACHING (during which my poetic production goes from 60 to 0), I feel rusty, irritable, and anxious to shift back into high gear as a writer. So, I invented a project for this transition: I would drive along the highways and write about exit-ramps, those places ravaged and recovered . . . as I hoped my ravaged self would soon recover. I had no overarching plan or theme. I didn't know how many ramps I would visit. My only rule was to observe, distill, crystallize my impressions, and then to create a form that might in some way mirror or reveal the exit-ramp's "content." I started at the Stowe/Waterbury exit and drove south, first along Interstate 89, then onward on I-91. Three days later, I had reached the Massachusetts border and had visited every exit along the way; thus began, in earnest, the full project, a chapbook's worth of poems called *Vermont Exit Ramps* (let's call it *VER 1.0*).

Exit 3: VER 1.0? So Vermont Exit Ramps II is a sequel?

YES, THE CHAPBOOK WAS PUBLISHED IN 2012 by Big Table Publishers in Boston. But there were still all those unvisited exits on I-89 north of Stowe and all of the exits on I-91 north of White River up to the Canadian border at Derby Line. So, back I went onto the road, and this time, I took a photographer with me, my friend Tony Reczek, whose photographs have graced the pages of *Vermont Life, Vermont Magazine*, and elsewhere. We retraced the exits of my original project, then pushed on to new territory over the next few years, shooting photos and writing new poems, always in the month of May—the month I'd launched the original project.

Vermont Exit Ramps II (or *VER 2.0*, as Tony refers to it) reprises some of the old poems—a baker's dozen of them from the chapbook—and then adds twenty-seven new ones. And, of course, this time, there are the gorgeous photos. We begin again with I-89, Exit 10 (Stowe/Waterbury). That's not arbitrary, by the way: simply, I live in Johnson, Vermont, and my access to the highway begins there. Let me tell you about my first day writing these poems. I was parked at the Stowe exit, pulled far off Route 100, and I was drafting my first lines and stanzas. Fifteen minutes into the process, flashing blue lights appeared in my rearview mirror. A police officer approached the car and asked why I was parked on the side of the road. So I told her: "I'm writing exit-ramp poems, officer." And I showed her my handiwork. "Would you like me to put you in one of the poems?" I asked. Though she declined, she seemed amused. At least she didn't give me a traffic ticket. Instead, she gave me advice, listing the rules of the ramps: no pedestrians allowed on the exit-ramp tarmac or on the cloverleafs of land nearby! No pedestrians, hitchhikers, animals, farm vehicles, snow machines. Nothing but proper, motorized vehicles, humming along on their way elsewhere! Well . . . she probably saved me from future traffic fines, so I thanked her, asked if I could stay where I was, and she said, "Yes, for a little while, but not for too long. Let's say, only as long as it takes to write a poem, which can't be too long, right?" Right . . .

Exit 4: When you wrote these poems, was your focus solely on exit ramps and the life inhabiting/surrounding them, or did it evolve in some way?

At first, I was only interested in observing, moment by moment, the natural world around each exit; one might call it *the habitat of the ramplands.* Once I turned my attention to the human impositions on the land, I began to think about how time alters both natural and human worlds. And I began to focus as much on the past as on the present (both the geological layers of Vermont granite, the ruination and recovery of the flora and fauna around these exits, and the human layers of history. I realized that each exit had a history, both public (which I could research in the nearby towns' historical records, using town halls, libraries, or Google) and private (my memories of traveling up and down these highways for forty years, often hitchhiking, often stranded at exit-ramps, often visiting friends and lovers in various towns nearby). Over time, a lot of the public and personal history began to inhabit these poems and bump up against the natural world descriptions.

Exit 5: Why do you juxtapose delicate landscape imagery with more banal descriptions of place?

I think of *VER II* as a book of post-pastoral poems. Vermont still has its bucolic pastures and hillsides, but the human population keeps growing, and it demands more consumer goods, boxy malls, bigger houses, faster roads, and all of the rest of it that bedevils us in this late-capitalist culture. So I consciously balanced the poems' pastoral lyricism with more deplorable details. I wanted a palimpsest of American history, from the primeval (granite, before ferns, virgin timbers) to the plasticization of modern culture. Each exit features a small world of earth and pavement, wires, signs, and other detritus that Americans have an intimate acquaintance with but give scarce thought to, but the *ramplands* also feature the ever-recovering wild and beautiful grasses, flowers, and trees. The poet delivers reportage about Vermont in the twenty-first century, but we know where his heart lives: along the wayside with nurturing green ferns, "something not under enormous pressure for millions/of years to perform in our fuel tanks . . . / something alive, present, nimble in sunlight/and shadow," as I say in the exit-ramp poem about Middlesex.

Exit 6: You have a date and time stamped on many of these poems, especially the ones highlighting the exits off I-89 and I-91; did these arise from a single trip or did they develop over time?

THE POEMS GREW OVER A FIVE-YEAR PERIOD in which I visited and re-visited each exit, accreting new material from observation, research, memory, invention, and constant reevaluation. As Robert Frost once said, "What begins in delight ends in wisdom." What began for me as a lark, driving the Vermont highways and recording observations of these *ramplands* on a glorious series of days in May, ended in a weightier consideration and collage of flora and fauna overlaid with human impositions, historical perspectives, and personal memories, all the while maintaining, I hope, some sense of linguistic play. I very consciously combined poetic modes and tones—narrative, lyric, collage; abstract commentary accompanying thick description; news reportage mixed with poetic tropes; serious scrutiny mixed with tomfoolery; factual history mixed with invented "facts"—all of which mirrors, or brings into focus, I hope, the complexities of 21st century Vermont.

Exit 7: Were there underlying themes you hoped to explore in these poems to unify the book?

I DID NOT CONSCIOUSLY TRY to achieve a thematic interplay between poems. I tried to be receptive to the specific interests and ideas each exit offered me in the moment of arriving there. If there are echoes between poems, it's because the same species of birds had arrived from their annual migrations and were singing on those specific May days; the same trees and flowers were in bloom. And the same consciousness (mine, with all of its desires and biases in tow) was responding to the stimuli of a spring day in Vermont. But each exit offered its own unique attractions and distractions. Some exits invited me farther afield, farther down the byways and into the surrounding towns, while other exits seemed to keep me close to the highway hillsides.

Exit 8: There's a lot of postmodern, tongue-in-cheek wordplay; how did these games with language arise?

I WANTED TO BALANCE INTENTIONALITY with serendipity in these poems—after all, so much of what happens, historically, is a matter of chance overlaid on human intention. I'm often worried about strong-arming a poem with too many preconceived ideas—as you can see I've done with these poems! Especially when I'm immersed in a subject that requires or promises research—oh, joy! Googlemania!—I can become unbearably referential, wearing my erudition (rather than my heart) too visibly. So I was looking for ways to counter too much intentionality. Beyond my normal penchant for puns, I introduced another variable: I used an anagram scrambler to scramble the town names in two- and three-word permutations and snuck some of these into poems: (*Stowe* becomes *so wet* or *to sew* while *Montpelier* becomes *pee-lit morn* and *triple omen*). I also interspersed bits from highway signs (*Please Merge Early*) and bought fortune cookies at Chinese restaurants near these exits, and I selected several fortunes, at random, to slip into each exit-ramp poem. So each rampland has a secret code and a forecast for its future. But enough of that!

As for the photographs, I'll let them speak for themselves on these pages. It remains to be said that without my friend and photographer, Tony Reczek, along for the ride, this project would have stalled out long ago. My deepest gratitude is to him, to my editors Tamra Higgins and Dede Cummings, who have devoted so much time, energy, and critical acumen to this project, and, lastly, to my partner in love and travel, Kate Riley, who read every poem, viewed every photo, and offered her wise counsel to make *Vermont Exit Ramps II* a stronger book.

May 2015, Johnson, Vermont

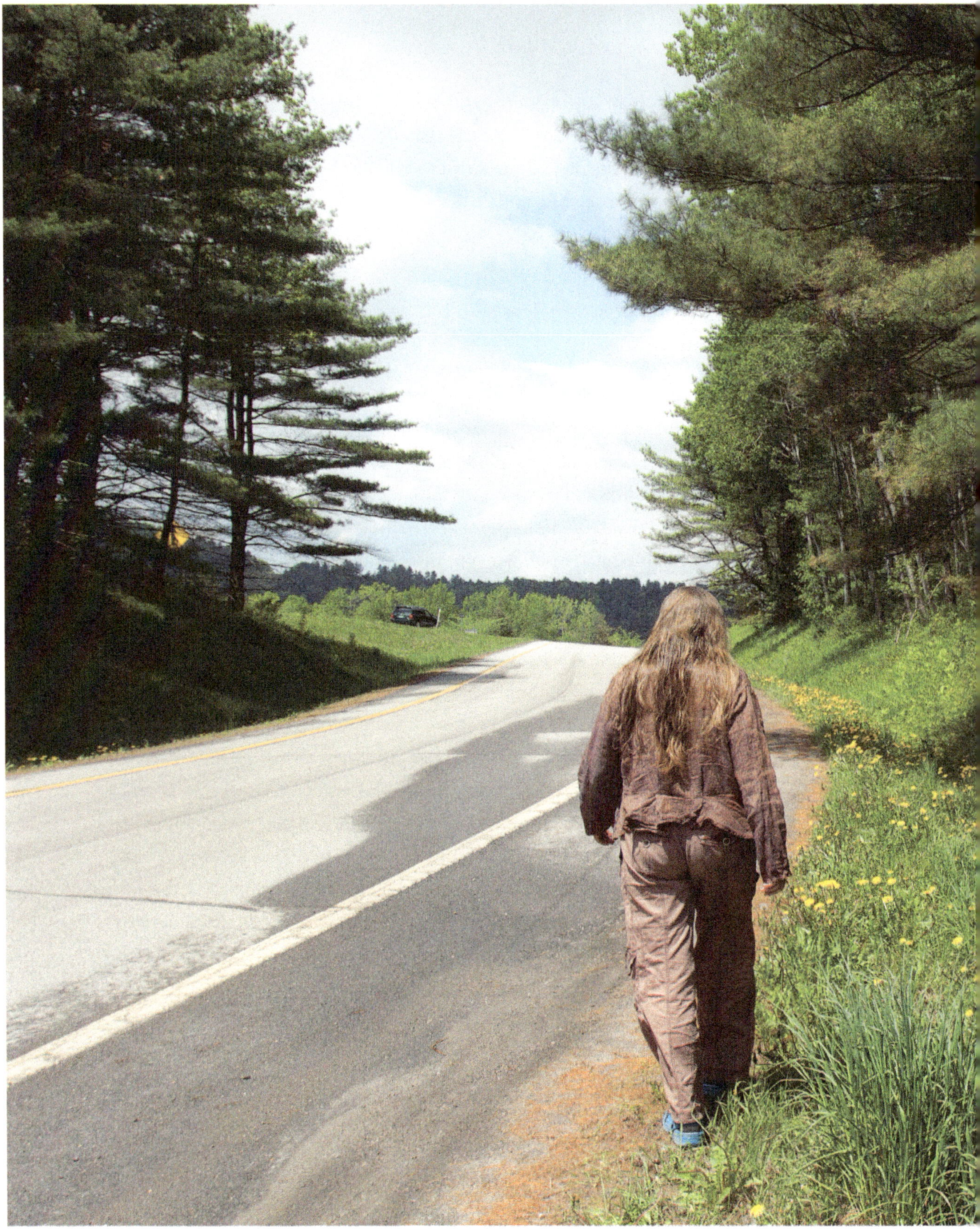

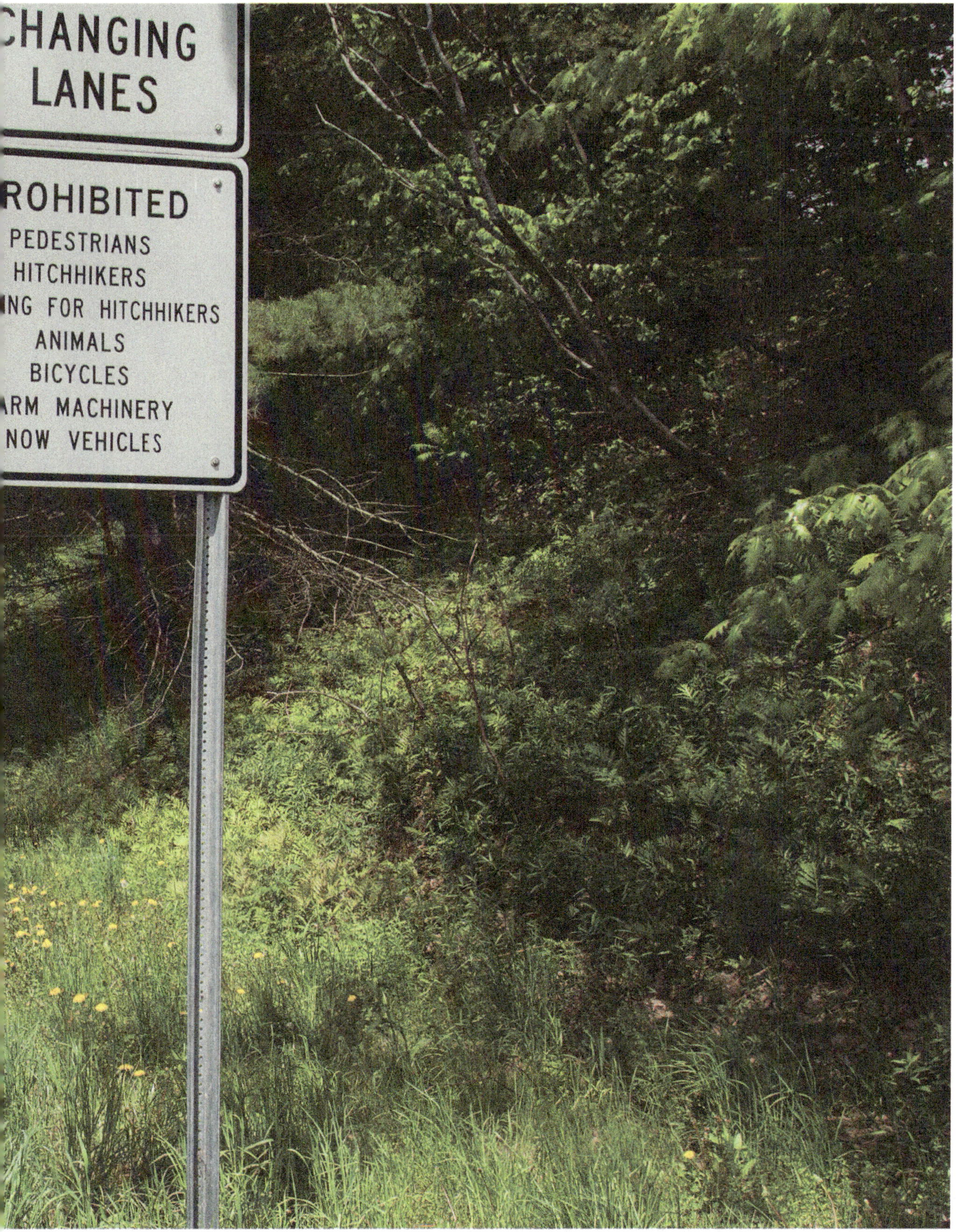
CHANGING
LANES
ROHIBITED
PEDESTRIANS
HITCHHIKERS
NG FOR HITCHHIKERS
ANIMALS
BICYCLES
RM MACHINERY
NOW VEHICLES

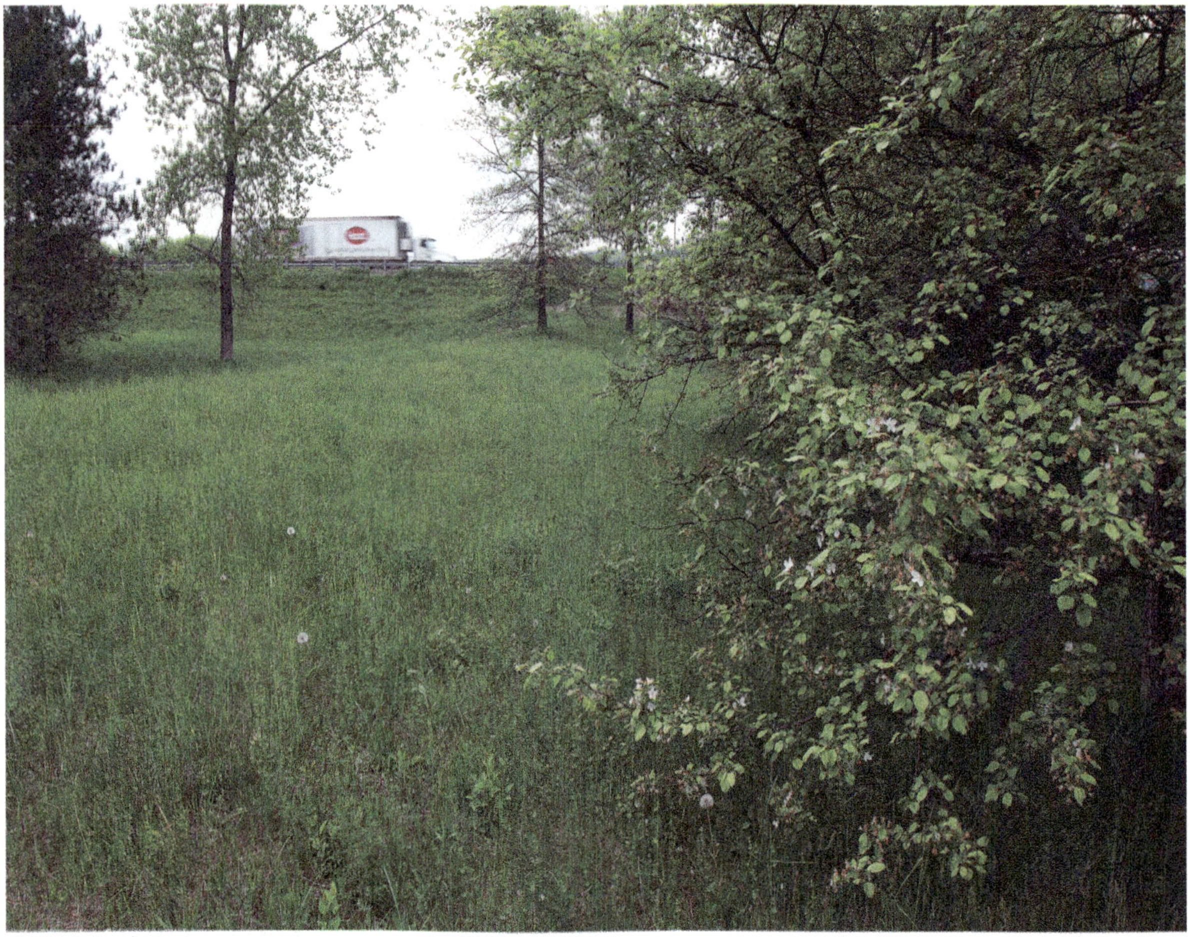

VERMONT EXITS

Who will claim the kingdom of exit ramps and cloverleafs
on the hillsides of I-89, these realms of birch and pine

rippling in mountain wind on a spring day, domains of quiet
forgetfulness, places ravaged and recovered—

these little demesnes of bedstraw and clover
harboring deer and bear, who stare at cars

grinding past, a driver's hands crossed around the curve,
a driver's mind attuned to the bend and merge

of traffic motoring down hillsides to the towns—
perhaps a deer lifts its head from grazing, its jaw

grinding sideways, its ears alive to the downshift of gears
or simple wind along the ridgeline, beech leaves scratching

over moss and duff. You might slow or stop here
for a quick piss or a picnic of wood sorrel and ribgrass,

young dandelion and fiddlehead, or you might imagine
a small cabin of clay and wattles made,

claiming this place no one claims, the heavy machinery
having rattled past and gouged a pasture elsewhere.

I-89, EXIT 10: STOWE/WATERBURY (Route 100)
May 18, 11:00 a.m. Full Sun

Blasted through fifty feet of granite
to make this exit "Vermont"
for tourists. *Unless you believe,*
you will not understand. What don't
we know? The history behind
every opportunity. The swelled
chests of road crews *so wet*
their sweat drips into hot tar.
The burned shoulders, explosives,
divorces from long days laying road.
Never mind. Your assignment is
to sew a story together. Delicate
hands, but the thread must be strong.
Your assignment is history, the Summit
House built as the Civil War broke out,
the Toll Road to the top of Mansfield
finished in 1870, the Big Hotel
that swelled across downtown,
burned to the ground in 1889.
Movement is another exit
down the road. Elsewhere, we say.
This history has snow in it and a Swedish
family in 1913 who swished through town
on long, narrow, wooden boards
with upturned ends. *The locals*
took to this strange transportation,
and skiing found a home in Stowe.
This history has a moneyed glide,

a schuss through powder, a hot-
tub view and a gold club perched high on a hillside.
Beneath it, loggers felling trees on a ski slope,
road crews with sledgehammer, pickaxe,
demolition dynamite. This history
has architect upon architect drawing plans
before the plans you produce in the space
of a poem. Granite before you thought
of granite. Granite before the dynamite
blast, before the tourist-idea: *Best*
Western Café Grill, Blush
Hill Country Club, Stowe
Street Emporium. ATM.

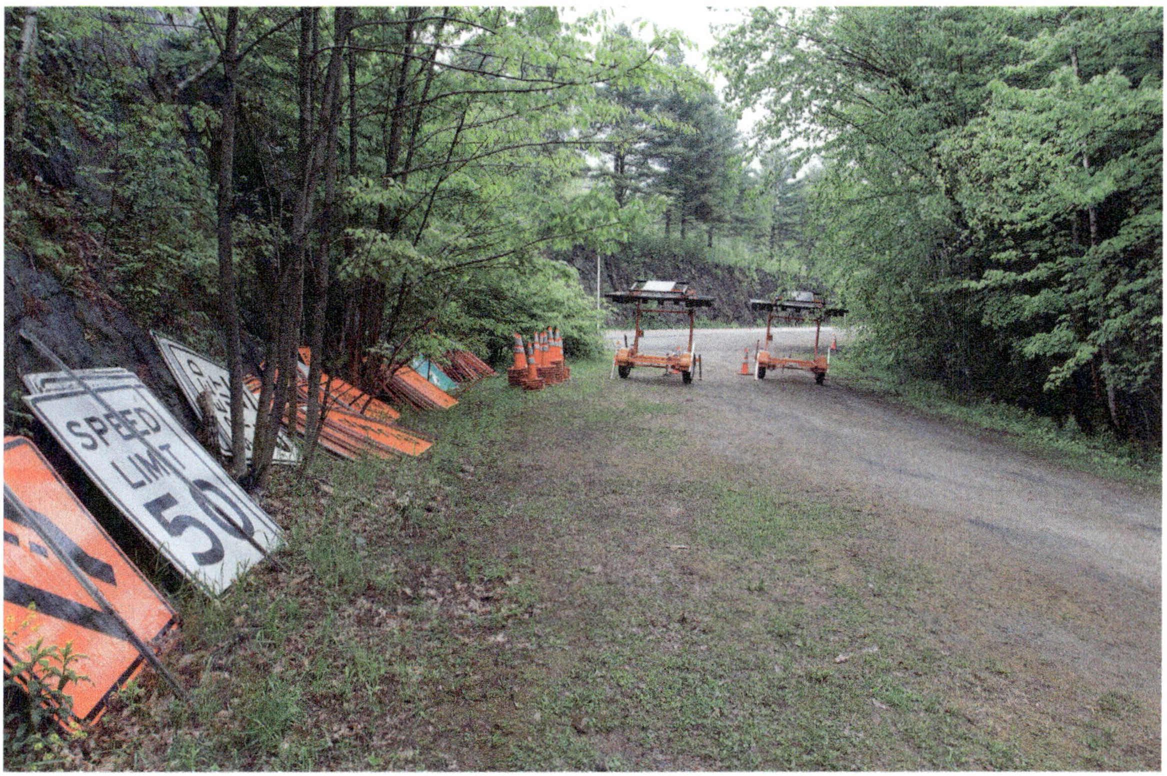

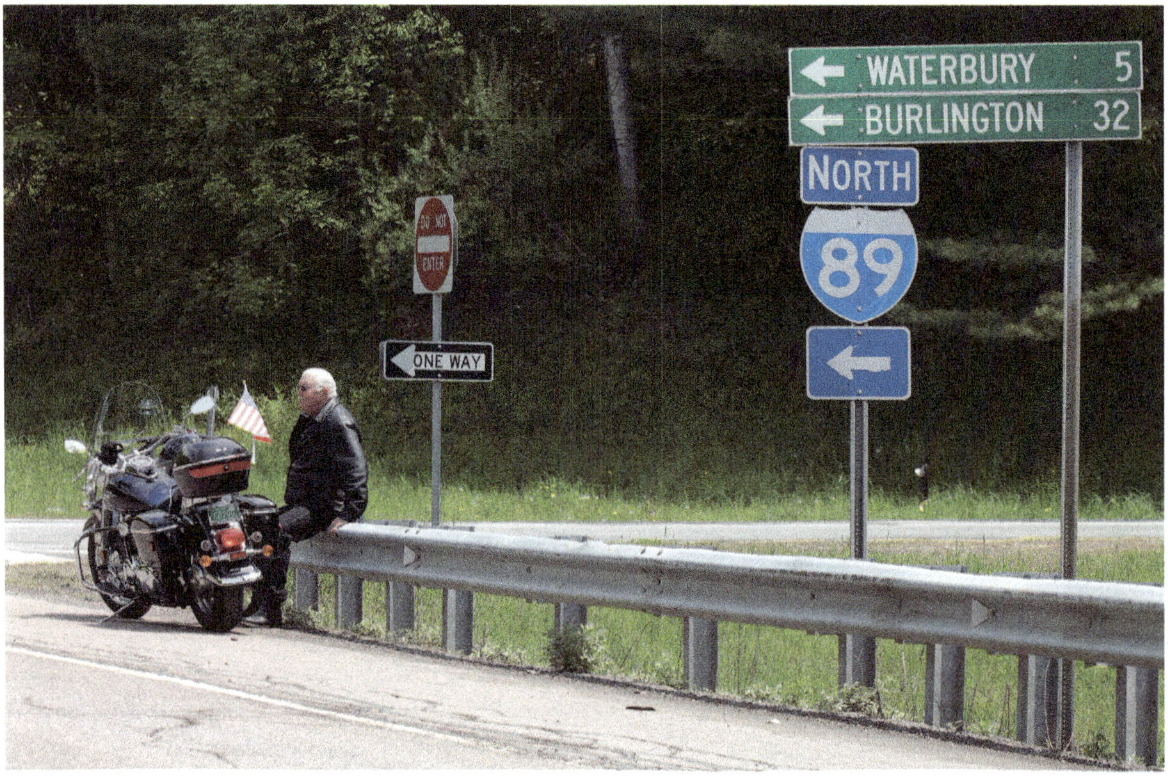
WATERBURY 5
BURLINGTON 32
NORTH
89
DO NOT ENTER
ONE WAY

I-89, EXIT 9: MIDDLESEX (Routes 100B, 2)

May 18, 12:30 p.m. Hazy sun, cloud build-up
"Middlesex, Moretown, Waitsfield, Warren, this exit"

So-so-so-so-sweet, yellow warblers call as you pull off
the exit ramp, going south. *Disappear into trees*
the breeze whispers. Highway above whispers
Goodyear Tires. Train-tracks rusting in a gulley below
murmur *Pacific Steel.* Is this *The Exit*
Time Forgot, lost between Stowe and Montpelier?

Turn right and meet the road to ski towns–
Waitsfield, Warren–where tourists seem *melded*
six thick, where everything is *sexed mild.*
Turn left and meet *Through Way Ends Here,*
a few cars, a few bicyclists pushing uphill
into trees and breeze and birdsong.

Legal Load Limit: 24,000 pounds. Pavement ends
in one mile, whether you turn right onto Brook Road,
where the locals do *mixed sled* in winter, right next to
the sign for *Ed's* (Famous) *Sled Mix,* or head straight
uphill to Middlesex Center Cemetery. *One generation*
plants the trees, and another gets the shade.

Push farther and you're in the Worcester Range, into
roads only locals know: Shady Rill where a Baptist Church
burned in 1849, Bear Swamp where a sheep farmer
shot five bears a day to preserve his flock,
Tangletown, *a place so named because the woods*
are so thick and so alike that settlers reported

getting "all tangled up," lost for days. By the wayside,
north-facing ferns still coil like green questions,
south-facing ferns unfurl in full sunlight, stretched into
the most delicate lattice-work. I don't have a name for it.
If I did, it would mean *ahistoric*. Something before
Make hay while the sun shines. Before Fern

Meadow, Moretown, Center Street, Park & Ride.
Something not pressed into ExxonMobil oil.
Not under enormous pressure for millions
of years to perform in our fuel tanks. Instead,
something alive, present, nimble in sunlight
and shadow, an energy-dance for our eyes.

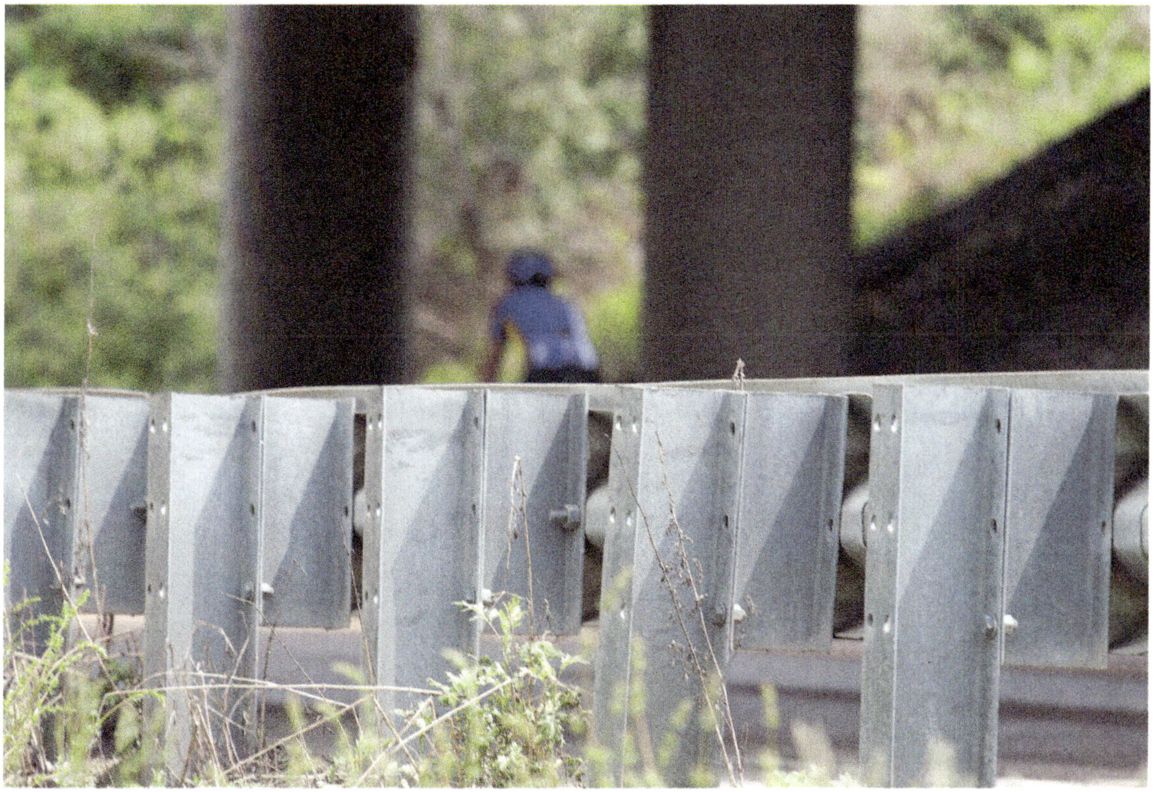

I-89, EXIT 8: MONTPELIER (Routes 2, 302)
May 18, 1:45 p.m. Hazy sun, clouds

Capital exit ahead. Gold dome. Every capitol mind is
a mind in progress, for progress, until it's not. Pet
project for the Interstate: *Mile Rent Ops* for new
billboards, the ban be damned. We need to fatten
our calves and our coffers! *Many a false step*
is made by standing still! Well, let's hope
politer men prevail. Today, the Winooski swells
with spring run-off, glinting below as you slow.
Bridge work. Please merge early. Merge
toward Montpelier, where *in-the-red* is ugly,
in-the-black beautiful. Merge toward a name
that's contraction and contradiction:
mont / peller: shorn hill. Really,
it's a glacial bowl, half-empty, half-full,
depending on the plumbing of the Water Works
on Dog River Road to keep the affluent
from the effluent. That's where farm run-off
meets town run-off. That's where suburbs
end. On that road, a tractor wobbles along, hauling
a fertilizer-spreader, an enormous mutt perched
on the tailgate. At the last stop-sign of the last suburban
curb-cut, it lifts a leg into the *pee-lit morn.*
Relieved. Toward what piece of backwoods
are they retreating? Montpelier lost its last
clothespin store in 2007, the last in America
before it burned. Today's primary business is fire
and life insurance. And government. Senators
serve best who bring home the bacon, the dairy

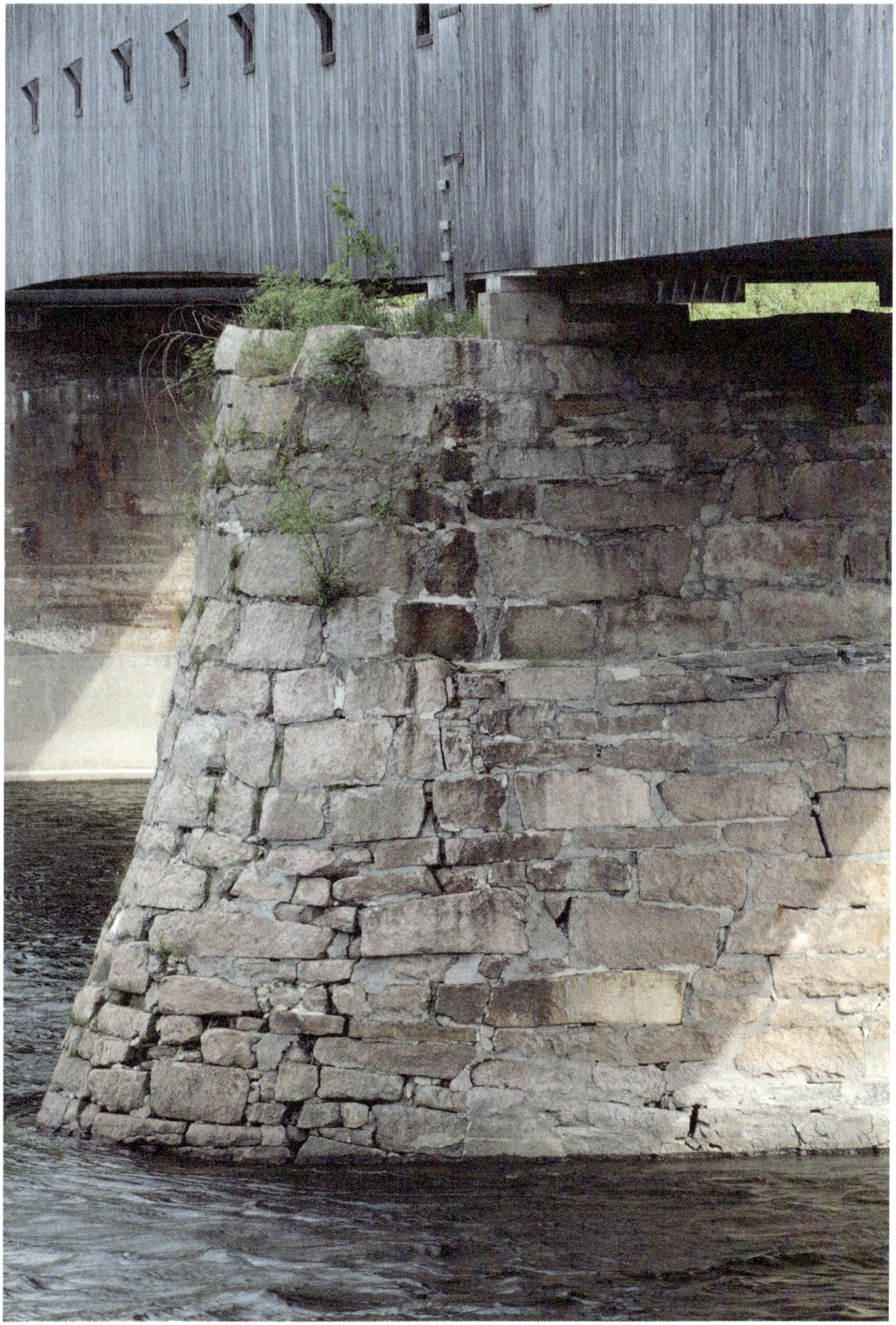

subsidy, the maple syrup tariff. To reach them,
follow the guardrails off the ramp, like centurions
of some processional, formal columns and great walls
of granite guiding you down. No place to stop
and consult the map before the force of the long curve
turns the steering wheel in your hands–the build-up,
bank, pressure (*triple omen*)—and suddenly
you're straightening out, gliding into the capital
with a swelled river, a glistering dome,
a library with a copy of the frieze from the Parthenon,
and signs planted all over town: *Keep the billboard
ban. Vote the Progressive Party!*

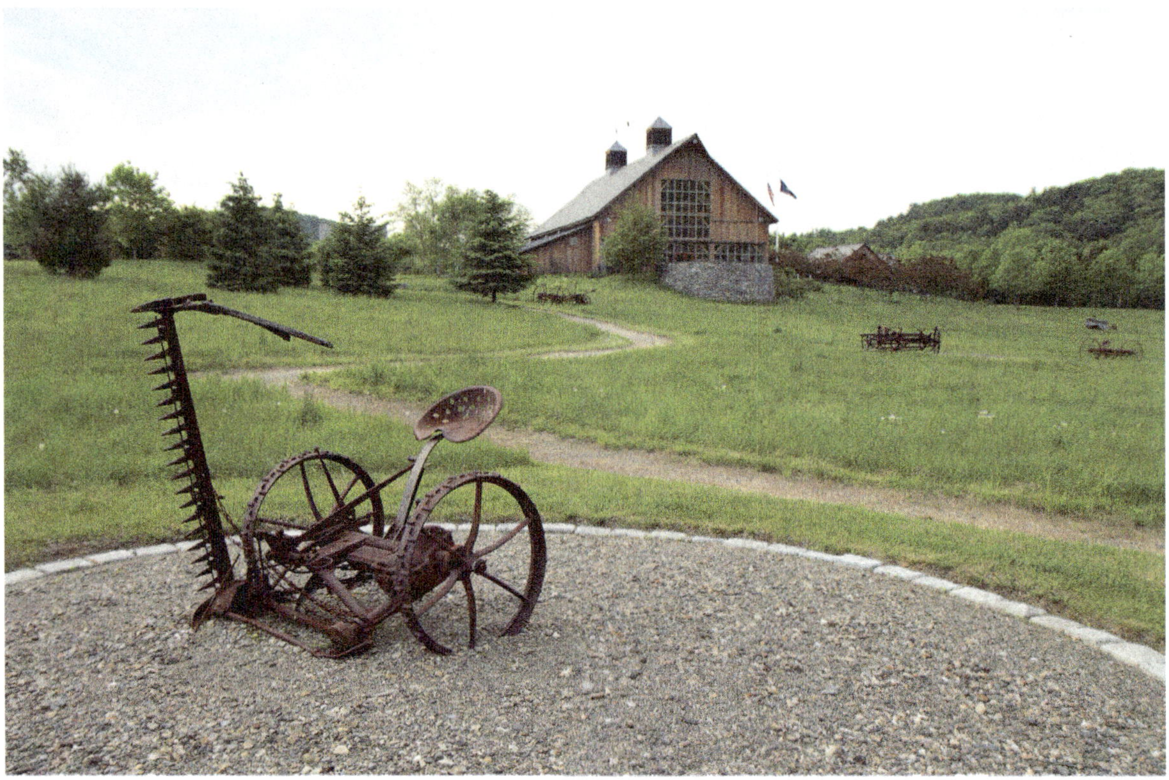

I-89, EXIT 7: BARRE/BERLIN (Routes 62, 302)
May 18, 2:30 p.m. High overcast
"Shopping, Goddard College, this exit"

These are the high exits of regret, six miles of switchbacks
descending to the backed-up traffic of downtown Barre.

Someone regretted its birth-name–*Wildersburgh*–changed
by civil vote or secret handshake–to *Barre*.

Only one way down these hillsides, going in the direction of excavation—
deposits of granite ten miles deep. Came the immigrants, men of stone,

from Italy and Scotland, Sweden and Spain, Greece and Lebanon.
No human leisure at this ramp—despite the golden cattails

in a culvert, gullies of birch and beech, private spaces
of marsh marigold—no amble, but full throttle on a banked turn.

Great-grandkids of these granite-men still work in granite—
the quarries, the cemeteries, the capitol hallways—and they burn

their wages in the bars and bowling lanes. On week-ends,
they burn it in snow-machines and ATVs. There are other ways:

Off the exit, six miles to the Berlin mall, hospital, or airfield,
they can shop or drop or fly away, three diversions from the day.

(Or go back upslope to that slim margin of trees, blackbirds wheezing
in the cattails.) Never mind. There's Applebees and Staples, Comfort

Suites and Shaws, Honda and Mobil. The names we give ambition. High
overcast. Squint weather. Crow's feet grow. Everything suspicious.

Ye who live and die by these franchises. Further afield, Plainfield
and trippy Goddard College (back in the '60s kids came naked

to the Governor's address, *barer* was better, *re: bra*-less), almost
closed now, their undergrads gone off to Wharton or Harvard Law.

Somewhere out there, I remember a used furniture store, dead center
Plainfield. Inside, the air's centuries old—at least the furniture is—

and you move in pockets of dust, thatched Shaker chairs, angel
beds, archebancs, hand-carved rocking horses, and no self-

serve at $3.99/gallon. No *Open on Sundays* burying the Blue Laws. . . . Snapped
back by blue Gortex riders buzzing by on lightning-blue Suzukis,

turning into Staples—for staples? Or will they get their staples at Shaws?
Where can I shop for a phrase that means "ruined future"?

Can a name-change make it all go *Wildersburgh* again?
How about a lane-change? *Left lane must turn left.*

Must right lane turn right? Right into the *rebar*. No *Park & Ride* for me, please.
I'll take the solitary pull-off spot. Across the way, Poulous Insurance. For insurance.

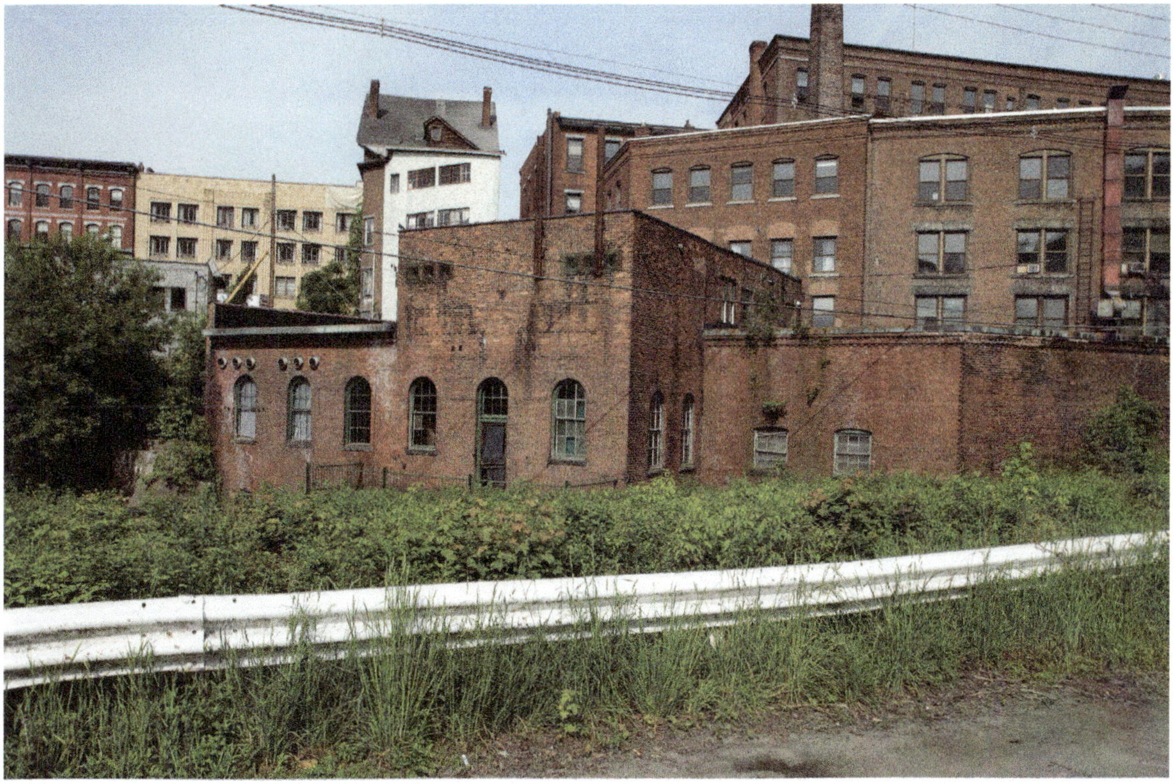

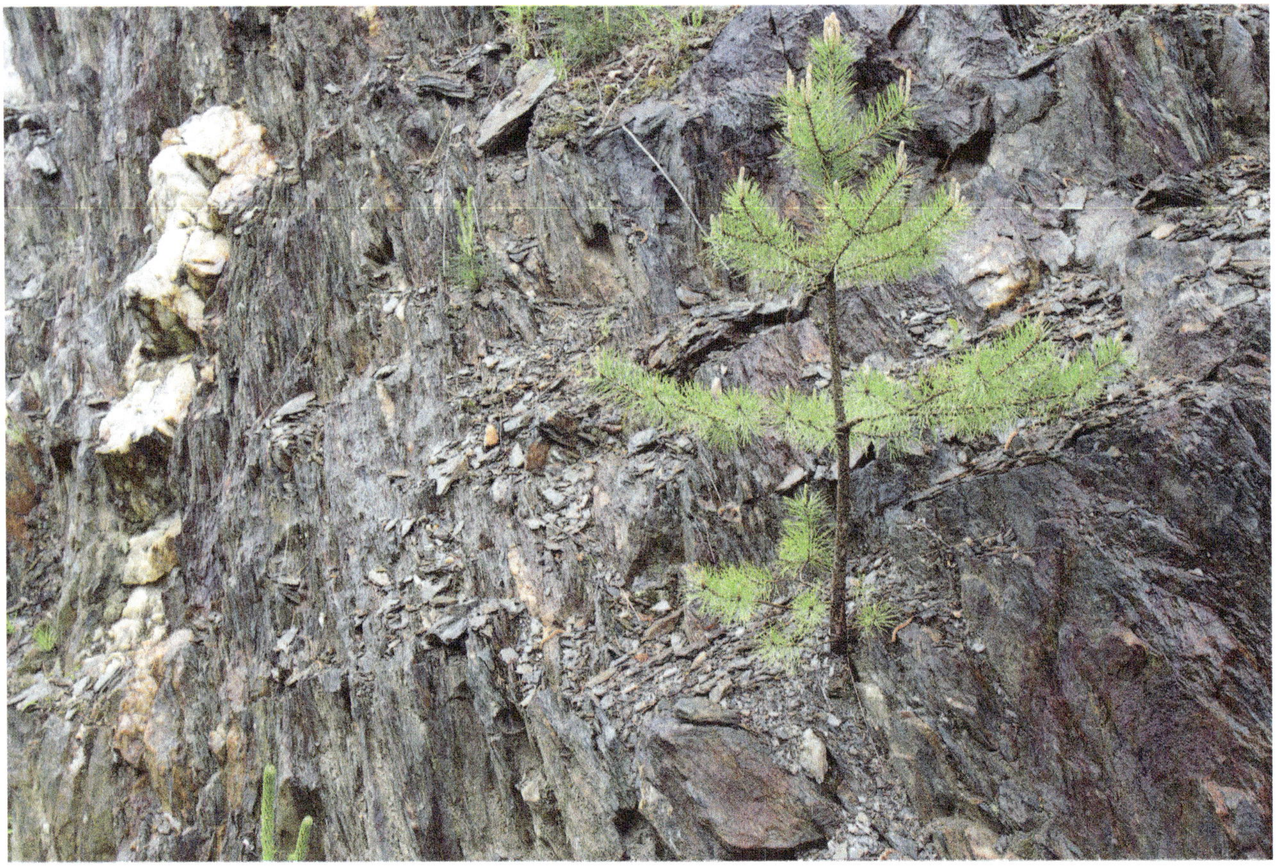

I-89, EXIT 6: SOUTH BARRE (Routes 63 to 14)

May 18, 3:00 p.m. Haze, clouds

"Granite Quarries, next right"

Ravens loop the high air above this exit,
one of the wild settlements of Vermont . . . . Don't kill it
with a poem. Never mind, no one reads, except
the words in chiselled stone for *a burst hero*.
A pile of birch lengths stacked at the end of the glen,
as if someone's home. Where can I pull off legally? Nowhere.
Six miles the descent to the valley, and up the other side, the pyramid
mountain in the eastern distance. Out there,
brown dust, and the famous depths of Barre quarries,
granite drilled, dynamited, dragged away.
Clank, belch, and roar of steam shovel, bucket loader, dump truck.
He who throws dirt is losing ground. Here, a hilltop swamp,
balsam fir and cattail, wetlands with red-wing's wheeze,
swamp-sparrow's sewing-needle call. Under the overpass,
three massive cement pillars, culverts with white
PVC pipe to divert run-off. Beside it, sumac, yellow
birch, yellow sign saying *Merge*. A flatbed goes by hauling
an old stagecoach. What's my time zone? In 1810,
the basic work was saw mill, grist mill. Everyone poor,
everything moved with a wooden wagon. 1812, the first granite
carved from a quarry, hauled off with
a wooden wagon. Stone soup. Starvation. A full
century passed before richness came with the railroad,
and with it, a means of moving granite on a grand
scale–words chiselled in cemetery stones from Barre—
to wherever death required it. *He who throws dirt is losing*
ground to Barre. And they increased. It's *breath or us*.

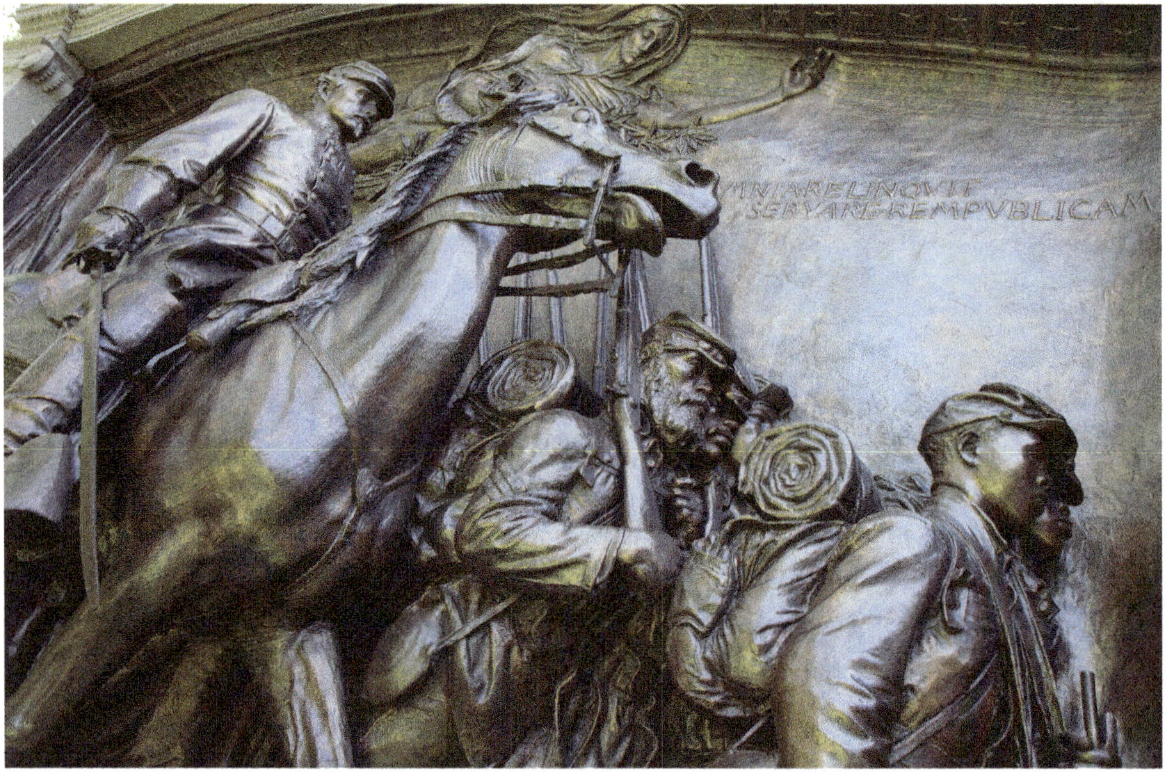
MNIA RELINQVIT
SERVARE REMPVBLICAM

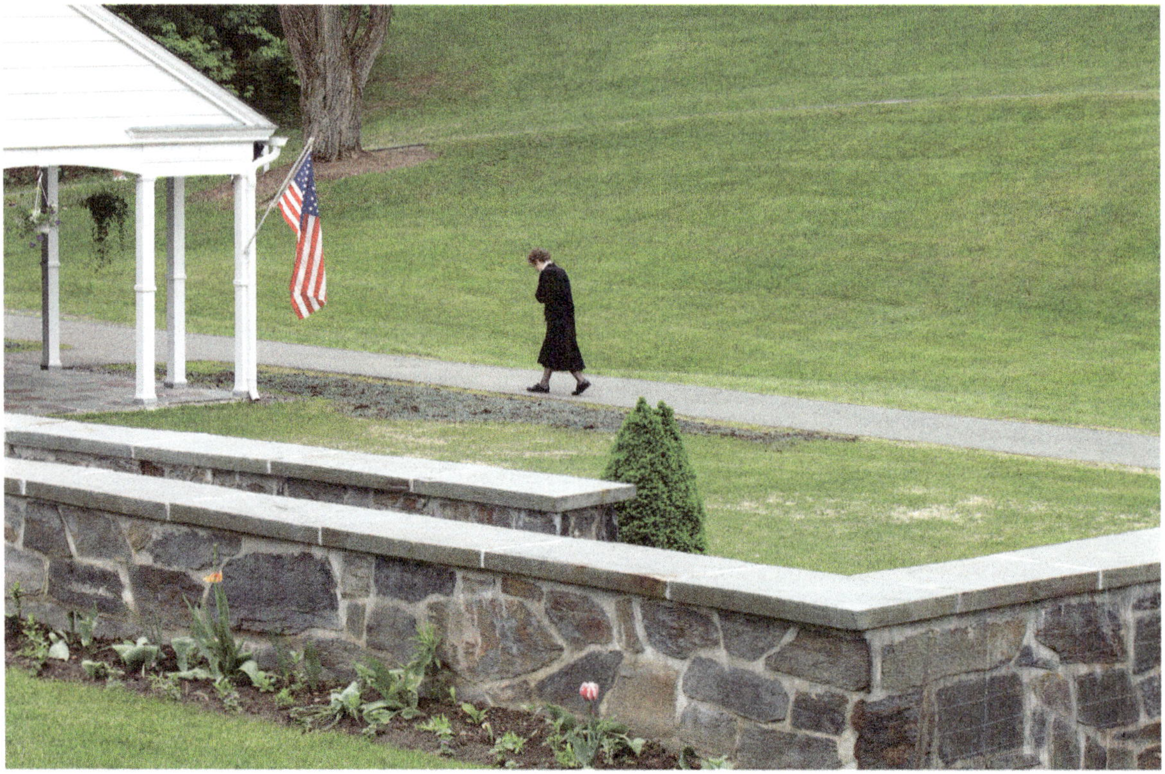

I-89, EXIT 5: NORTHFIELD (Routes 64 to 12)
May 18, 4:00 p.m. Full clouds
"Exit for Norwich University"

Flat exit through cut brush.
Ramp matter-of-fact. Arrive. Execute.
Leaden sky. Park & Ride. Busy on Sunday. Why?
Four buddies in a 4 x 4. Gas, $3.79.
First sound: gunshot. Target practice?
First sight: wire-mesh, keeping us
from what? These are the signs. Gunshots
go on and on. Norwich cadets on
an afternoon mission? Between gunfire,
the internecine chirr of blackbirds vie
for nesting sites. Swamp water pings
with rain. I'm out of steam, 4:00 P.M., the sun gone.

I'll need to face this town I've steered around
for years. (How many others have bypassed
its heady, military air?) Norwich has *held*
fort in this town since 1866, stuck here
like a *filed thorn*. First turn-off:
Glacier Valley Road. A site contested,
scraped to hardscrabble by retreating
knives of ice. Rock-fields. Stone-pickers.
A lone woman on the road, worrying
a hoop basket against her hip. To where?
From whence? *A woman who seeks to be*
equal to men lacks ambition, they say
in the training camps. A way of saying . . .
what? Further on, the steep descent

into Northfield, a runaway truck lane
up a steep incline, over which a cliff.

Now, Norwich University, full of four-
story white clapboards, smart conversions
of gambrel barns. Quads squared by sharp
brick-and-ivy dorms, classrooms. *The greatest
danger is hubris.* On the main street, crisp
colonials, American flags flapping out front.
What they say to Communists: *Red Filth, no!*
You can almost hear the *lifted horn* playing reveille.
In one yard, a headphoned teen executes
a four-square pattern on his front lawn,
listens to what? Punk rock? John Philip Sousa?
Marching orders he'll defy or obey? Above Norwich,
on a green hillside, a camouflaged Humvee
bumps down a mown path in misting rain.

I-89, EXIT 4: RANDOLPH (Routes 66 to 12)

May 19, 11:00 a.m. Sun and high clouds, crisp after a night of rain

There's something open and honest about the exit-
ramps of Randolph. A dozen miles divorce
us from the buzz and rumor of Barre. We climb
the highest highway elevations, cruise alpine meadows,
view white slashes on ski peaks, snowy exclamations
in May, spacious air all the way to Randolph—

There's nothing hidden here. (You called at midnight:
Still open for poetry if I arrive in an hour?) No glen or secret
wood. Everything plain and perfunctory—easy on/easy off—
(our bodies, primed, performed) with three willows swaying
in a green field. On the radio, Frankie singing, *On a clear day,*
you can see forever . . .

Above me, pasture sloped to the sky, (slope of your
shoulder) below me (cool linen) fields slanting down
to Randolph, and farther off (*please consider*
a penis-ring like Carl's) across a broad valley, the Braintree
Mountains. *On a clear day,*
you can see who you are . . .

Sun and puffy cumulus. (Lover's circles under our eyes) High spring
of apple blossom and bird song. Nearby, American flags flapping
over Mobil and McDonalds. (There's no allegiance
in your gaze; I don't require it.) Cross-street, banners announce
the grand opening of Three Stallions Inn Driving Range.
(You and I will be powering a few balls in an hour.)

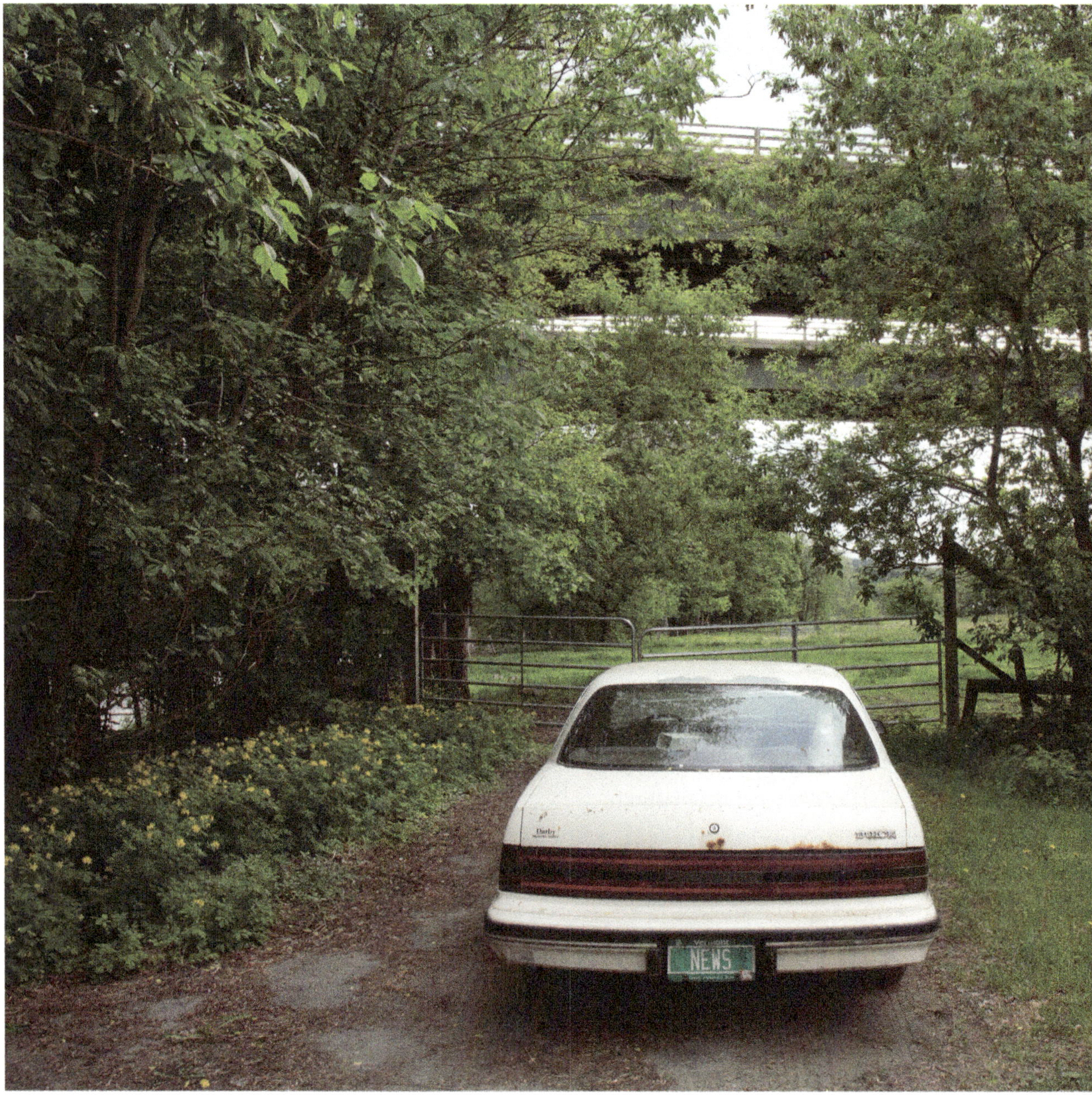
NEWS

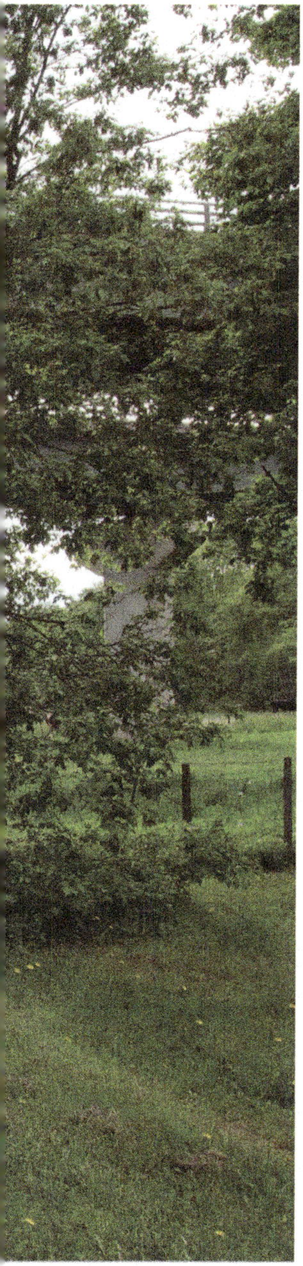

Yellow school bus and Lays Potato-Chip truck
flash by. (Salt in the throat) Another truck: Hoods/
Booth Brothers. Was it a milky merger? (Your
breasts spent) A high stakes takeover?
The digital road signs flash: *Road Work: Merge*
Early. Everything clear and foreseeable, framing

our expectations: *Expect Delays.* (How many
nights will I remain . . . until the penis-ring?) *On a clear day,*
how it will astound you . . . All the cards are on the table
in Randolph, the exit perched above highway, sensible,
direct, outward-looking. (Not like exits that disappear
under highway pilings, underworlds of intrigue

and interiority.) Take, for instance, the unencumbered
road uphill to Randolph Center, a home-made sign
on the lawn—*Home of Al Floyd*—welcoming you in.
(Or downhill, to your home, where the hot-tub's
bubbling, the hibachi grilling a few rib-eyes.
Don't over-think it, lover-boy. Here is

whatever you want.) You'll feel part of,
part of every mountain . . . Or downhill,
to the first sign of deception: the lone
Asian-fusion promising the impossible: mouth-
watering sushi, lemongrass soup,
or moo goo gai pan. And a fortune:

A conclusion is simply the place
where you got tired of thinking.

I-89, EXIT 3: BETHEL/SOUTH ROYALTON (Route 107 to 100/14)

May 19, 12:00 noon. Sun with cirrus
"Vermont Law School, this exit"

Exit into white lilac and thick apple blossom. Someone has money
for a royal welcome. *Pleased-pleased-to-meet-you*, says the Tennessee
warbler, and the yellow warbler in lilac answers: *so-so-so-sweet.*

Coast down a long incline to White River, concrete pilings
lifting the highway high above mudflats and oxbow-meander.
Down here, Perley Farm's in the valley of the shadow, almost

lost under the underpass, but its silver silo rises eye-level
to the interstate and stares it down: *Bet hell* and high-water
this farm survives! Just two exits here, not four, because of the river.

Just two cloverleafs. Everything just is: Perley Farm in shadow;
highway in sun. Hay-truck hauling bales, seven high, toward Bethel;
Volvo hauling lawyers to South Royalton. *Our snotty halo.*

Choose your justice: in Bethel, buildings crowd close to the street,
workers on humped sidewalks, opening a lunch pail and thermos.
As the purse is emptied the heart is filled. In South Royalton,

eateries face the fountain on the village green, clientele in suits
and ties. *Every excess becomes a vice.* A grand avenue opens
on the town square, Rockwellian train station, Victorian

offices of the Law School. Choose your justice. *So-so-so-sweet.*

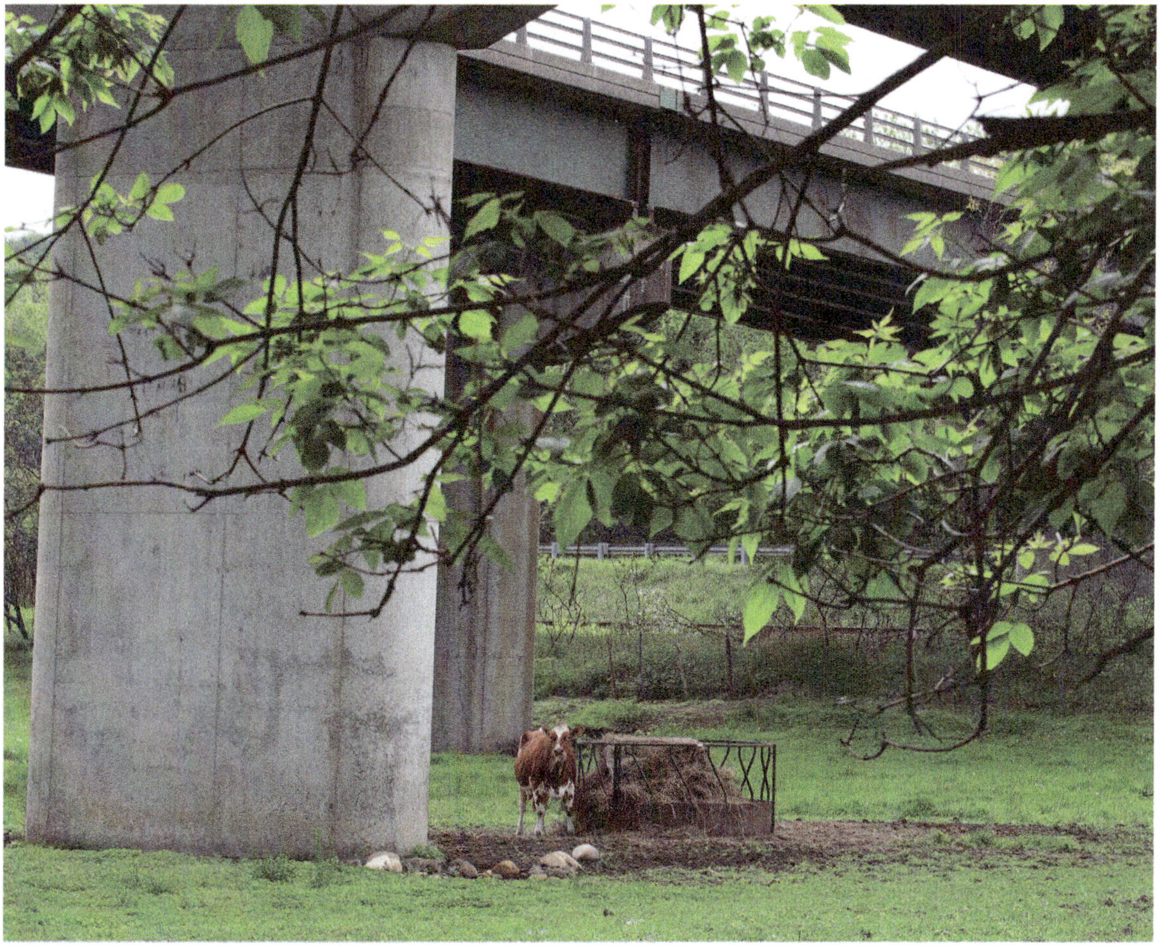

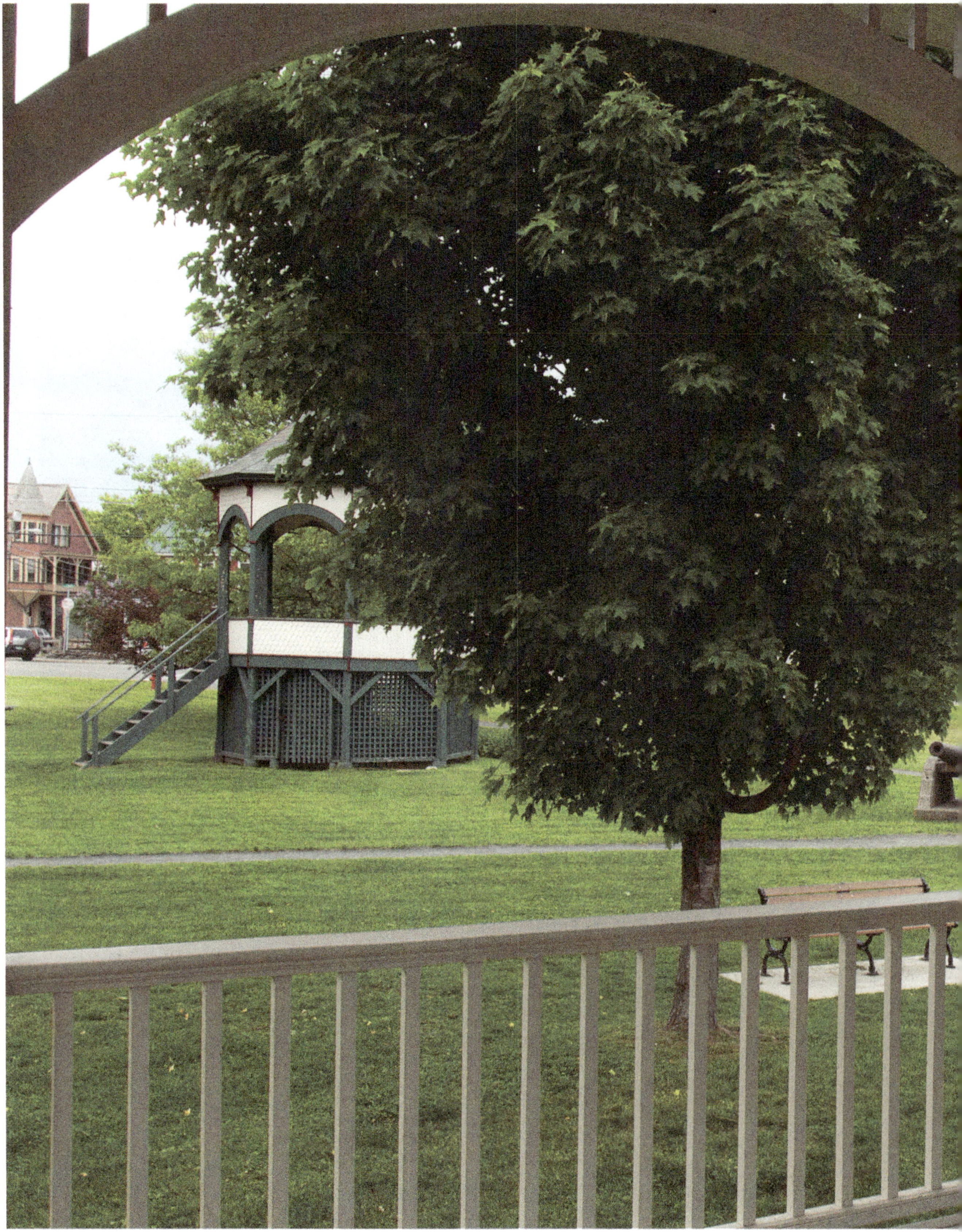

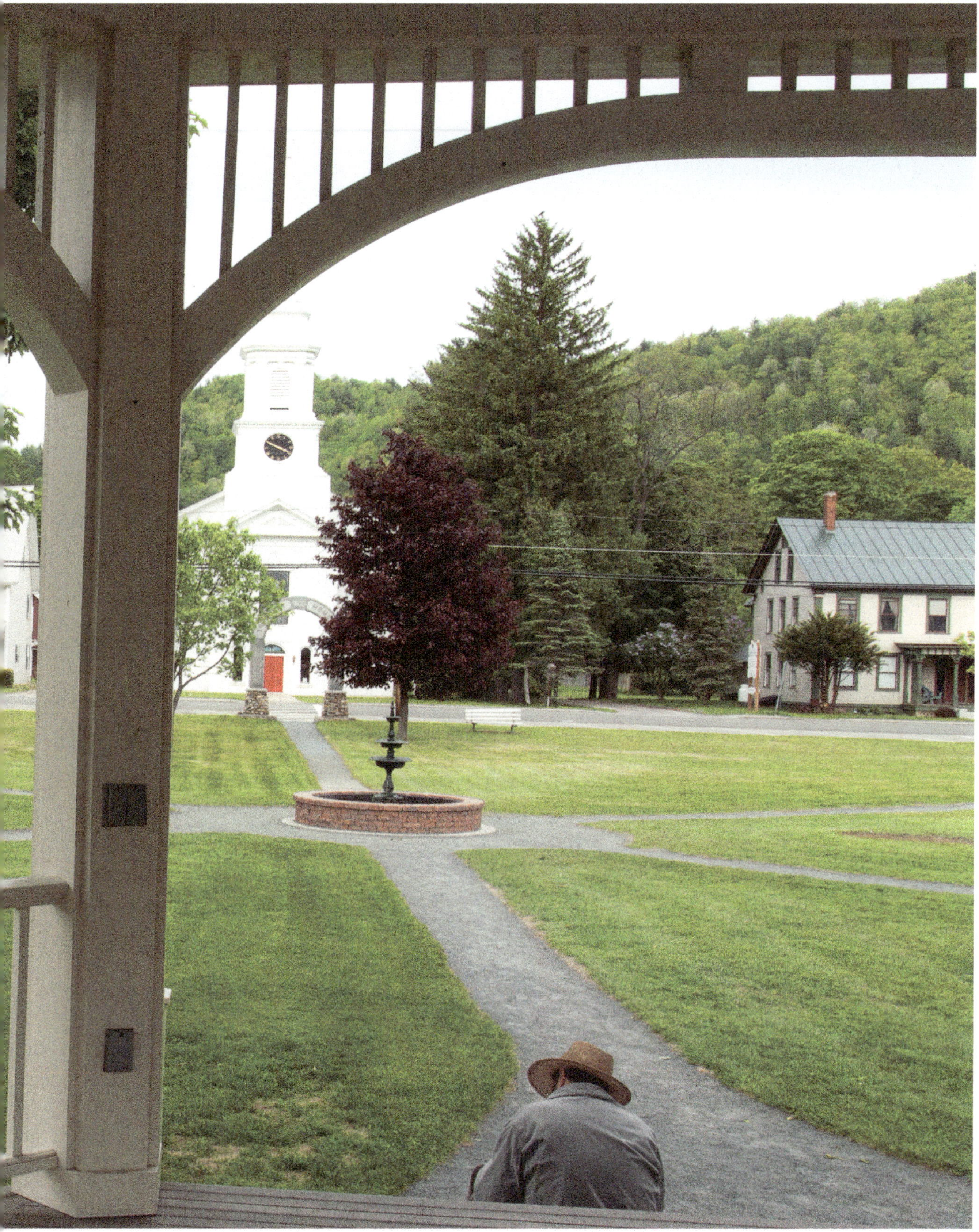

TOWN GREEN: SOUTH ROYALTON

How long has it been since I lazed on a town green?
(Wistfulness, beware.)

A couple of square acres set with maple and crab apple.
(Sprayed, mulched, blooming impossibly early.)

Two gazebos, for bandstand and romance.
(*Amo, amas. Gazebo, gazebae*?)

Starched white church with a black clock-face.
(The time is *what* ungodly hour?)

Across the green, a train station where business begins.
(End of the line.)

Before me, a *cottage row*; behind, a row of *eaterie*s.
(Who cooks in a chichi town?)

On its grass surface, not a weed or divot.
(No sliding tackles, scraped knees?)

From the highway, South Royalton seems tucked in timelessness
(a steeple crucifix, a gambrel barn's weathervane)

like a storybook town one sees from a passing car, wishing
(fairytales were true)

fairytales were true, wondering how one gets there
(from here)

from here. Forty years ago, I'd have lain
("loafed and invited my soul")

here on a summer's day, a college kid astride the season
(riding it, riding it)

tethered to greenness and leisure. Forty years ago,
(o lord)

o lord, in whose crossed steeple I do not believe, in whose name I cannot
(stop time)

claim hope or victory. Forty years, and my body still yearns
(for the idea of greenness)

for green.

I-89, EXIT 2: SHARON (Route 132 to 14)
May 19, 1:30 p.m. Sun, hazy high clouds

Sharon, oh Sharon. *A shorn* place. Neither *ash nor*
rash on you. *You're never too old to become*
younger. Sharon, full of sand steam-shoveled
from the hillsides. Below you, White River swirls,
three bridges to carry across its shallow meandering.

Sharon, river town, crimped on a curve
of the interstate, between river and humpbacked
hills, between something and nothing. Sharon, *a smile*
increases your face value. Your exits are
niggardly slices of land, little isosceles triangles,

cut between speedy highway and brake-light exit ramp. This is a short
visit, the one restaurant lost to arson, *convenience* store bankrupt.
Brake off the exit and stop at a school. *Teachers open the door,*
but you must enter by yourself. Commuter lot converted
to First Congregationalist Church. No one else to commute

or convert. This way to the aging Town Clerk (the demographics
don't look good), that way to a closed hotel, converted to apartments,
a sign *Vacancies*. This is the land of exhaustion and surrender,
a place for *Second-hand Furniture, Trading Post,* and *Danger:*
Falling Ice. The Mormon, Joseph Smith, was born here. He left

for multiple wives in Utah. There's a hand pointing → ATM.
Take your money, and run. Run, Sharon, run! O hopeless one
pressed between water and boulder, what is there to do
but walk out to the rocks, cast a long fishing line,
and hope for a tug from the river.

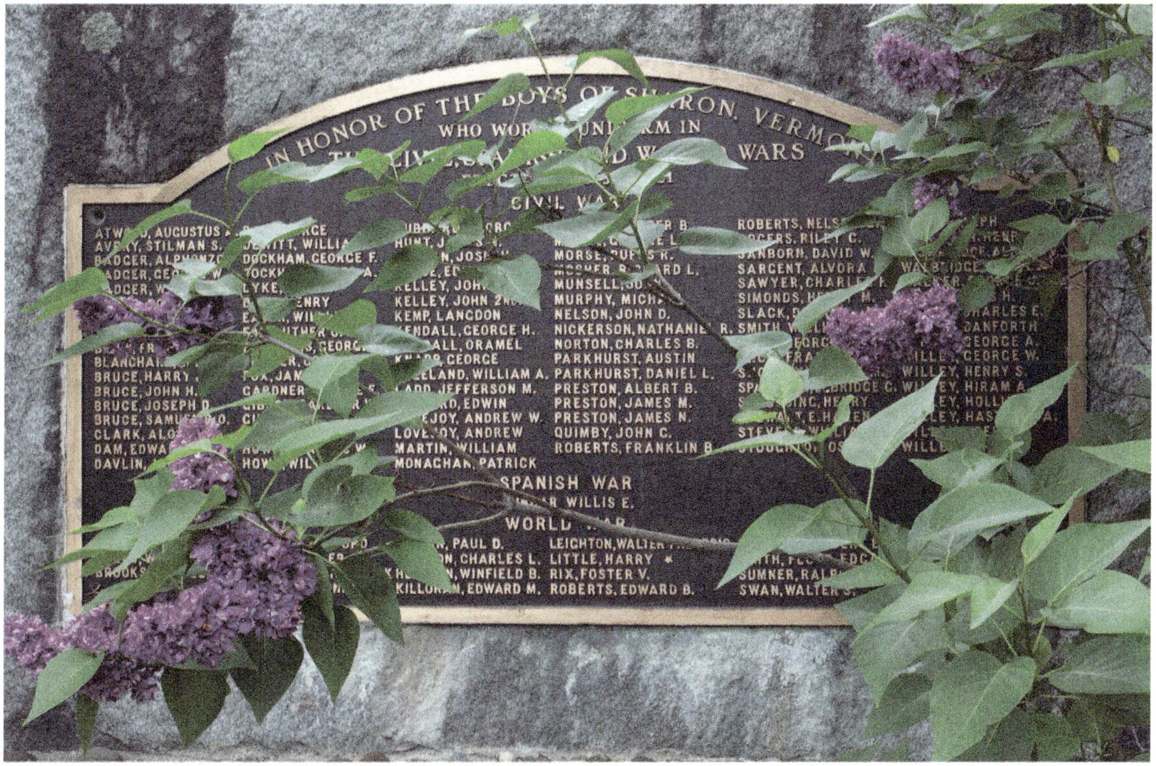
WARS
CIVIL WAR
BRUCE, JOHN H.
BRUCE, JOSEPH D.
DOCKHAM, GEORGE F.
KEMP, LANGDON
KENDALL, GEORGE H.
MURPHY, MICHA
NELSON, JOHN D.
NICKERSON, NATHANIEL R.
NORTON, CHARLES B.
PARKHURST, AUSTIN
PARKHURST, DANIEL L.
PRESTON, ALBERT B.
PRESTON, JAMES M.
PRESTON, JAMES N.
QUIMBY, JOHN C.
ROBERTS, FRANKLIN B.
MARTIN, WILLIAM
MONAGHAN, PATRICK
SANBORN, DAVID W.
SARGENT, ALVORA
SIMONDS
WILLEY, GEORGE W.
WILLEY, HENRY S.
SPANISH WAR
WILLIS E.
WORLD WAR
LITTLE, HARRY *
RIX, FOSTER V.
ROBERTS, EDWARD B.
KILLORAN, EDWARD M.
SWAN, WALTER S.

I-89, EXIT 1: WOODSTOCK (Route 4)
May 19, 2:30 p.m. Sun, haze

Strange, indeed, to drive down a winding exit so long . . .
estates, side-streets, a barking dog, and Mosely real estate
greet you before you turn onto the main road.

Perhaps you're buying property in Quechee—did I tell you
the one about the millionaire who drove her Porsche
off Quechee Gorge, totaled the car but lived to buy another—

or perhaps you're going all ten miles down the shadowy road
to Woodstock where Rockefeller dollars mix with Mafia,
and it's hail-fellow-well-met at Ye Olde Woodstock Inn.

If you don't behave, they'll break your fingers
and your piggy bank. (*Sock! Dot! Ow*!) Let's stay at the exit ramp,
dependable Mobil soaking up your simoleons, and besides,

Pegasus Gallery (the first of many on your way to art-happy
Woodstock) is open for business. *Words like "romantic"*
and "magical" are often used to describe this quaint village

that has been called "the prettiest small town in America."
I once loved someone there—is why I'm bitter—though
I dumped *her.* On its surface, like so many surfaces there,

it was about money: sugar-daddies and sugar-mamas
and marriages minted in hell. She had too much
sugar, and I didn't know what to do with it. *Do not mistake temptation*

for opportunity. A commercial truck flashes by from Quechee—
All Decked Out—does, I assume, decks. Why does capitalism run
on bad puns? *You'd be wise to invest your stock in Woodstock.*

Middle afternoon on a Tuesday, just before school buses muck up
the roads, flashing red lights, stop signs flopping out, kids descending
the steps. Did I tell you the one about the millionaire

who drove over a school-kid's dachshund? Shoved fifty bucks in his fist,
Go buy yourself another. Woodstock is a really nice town,
and the Village Book Shoppe carries all the local histories. Don't try

to read them—someone might break your fingers. Fiddlehead picking
is possible. The hills are thick with ramps and morels. And, of course,
loads of jolly pubs. Did I ever tell you the one—

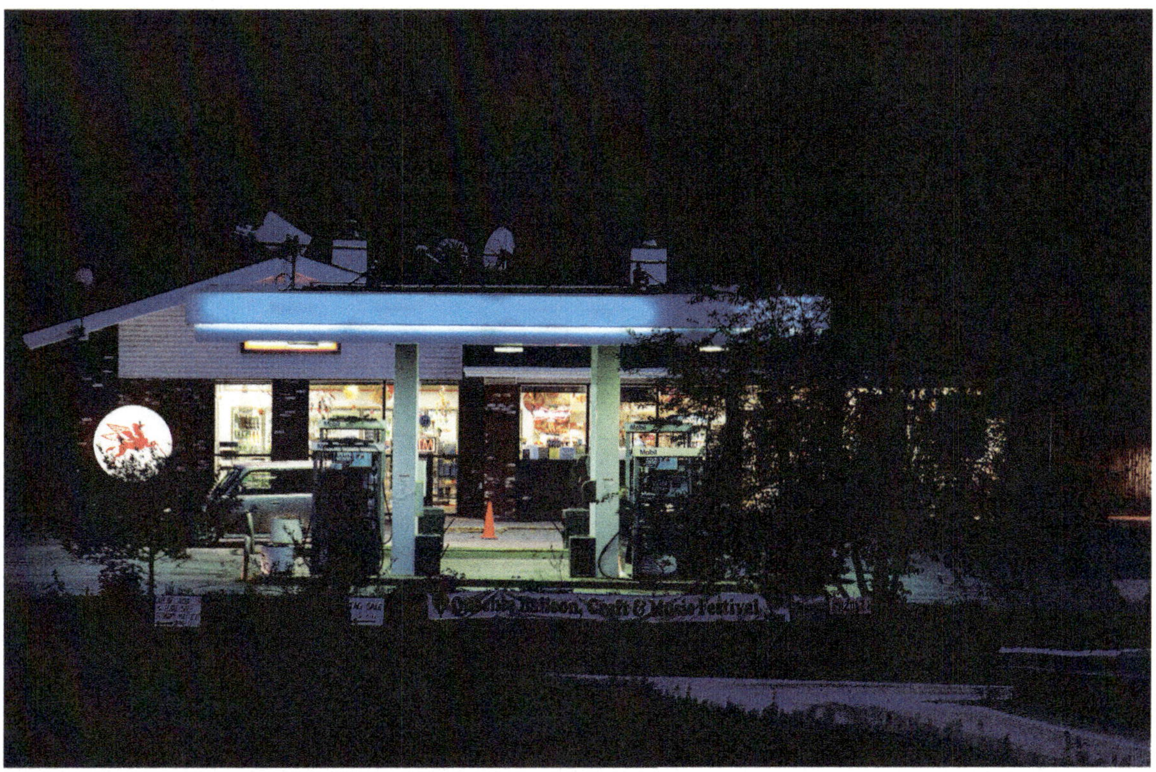

I -89: WHITE RIVER JUNCTION (Interchange I-89/I-91)
May 19, 3:00 p.m. Sun, high clouds
At the Rest Area/Weigh Station, one mile south of White River Junction

There's no getting off at the nexus of exits, high granite walls
conduits to other states, states of mind, nowhere to stop,

so go the extra mile to Rest Area/Weigh Station just south of White River
and weigh in. Which way to go? What are you doing, doing this, this drift

down the river of whimsy, your vim and vinegar? Refusnik poetics, poetics
of unimportance and neglected picnic spots? Weigh in. Where's the freight

you thought you were hauling? Hijacked fifty miles back? Never loaded
in the first place? *Logistics Equipped. Air Ride Equipped. SWIFT.* A parked truck,

a highway sign: *Click it or Ticket.* Hiss of airbrakes. Weigh in—even if this station isn't open.
Was it a lightweight idea? A radical announcement? A reclamation:

Of the fat, cigarette-smoking trucker in Hawaiian shirt walking his girlfriend back
from the bathroom. He opens the cab door, and she climbs in to *Yankee Trucks.*

Who takes his girl on the road? For him, something better than CB chatter?
A blowjob in the cab? For her, a string of love-songs on the radio,

a string of towns flashing by that are not her town. Fat transport, lighten
the load, however you see fit. Nearing 60, with too much philosophy

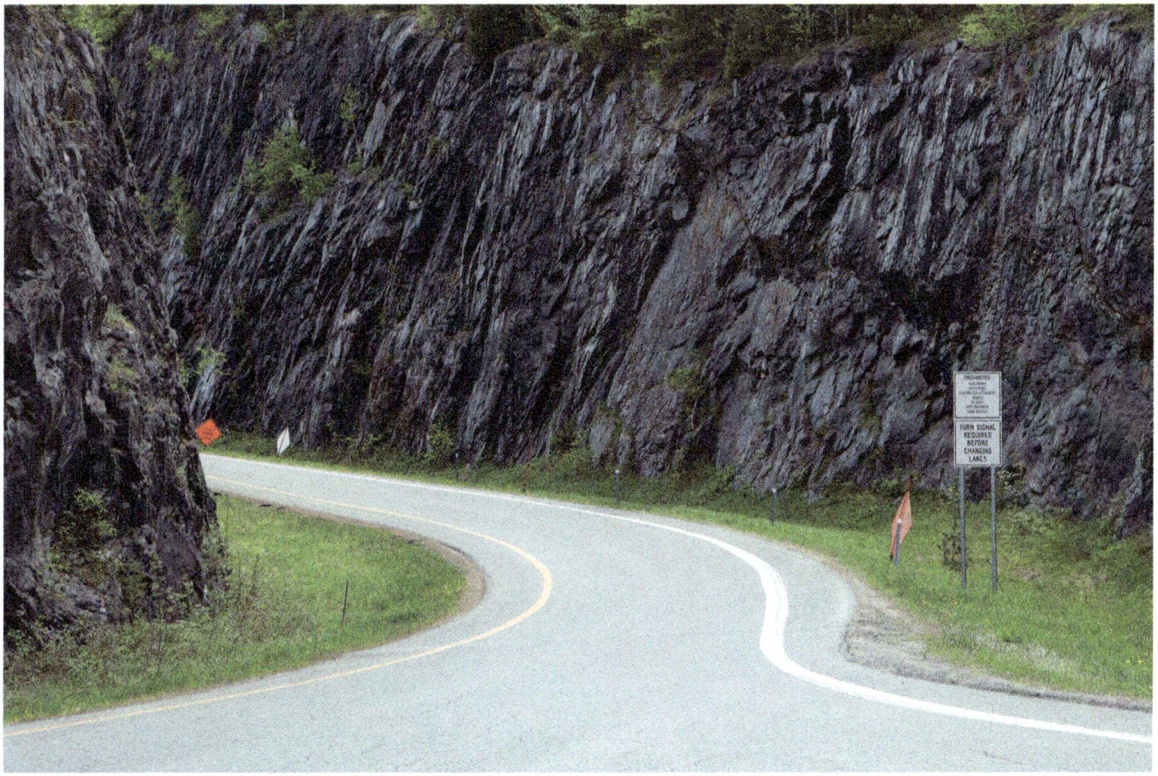

in your bones, and too much apocalypse, you're trying to carry the world's
heaviness like dandelion fluff, cottonwood spindrift—trying to turn

nexus of granite walls into something more than an endless transport,
no peace, no green, black canyon with a finger's width of sky. Trying

to turn the nexus of here and hereafter into an exit. Nexus of next act
and rest stop. Nexus of prosaic and lyric. *Please merge early.*

SECRET EXITS

Not the garments of a cross-dresser stashed
behind a wood pile. Not the blood-soaked shirt
of a missing girl. Not even soggy wallets
dropped in a hasty tryst. Not a human thing.
Just pasture carved into cloverleafs, ramplands recovering
their purpose, which is to grow whatever green things
plant themselves here. Better still, if a little mossy hill
full of forget-me-not or hawkweed, a deep declivity
of beech and hazel-wood, a stand of white pine or
birch ringed by rain-gorged mushroom . . .
Anything private and islanded, untended
by human hands, unintended, and unattended.

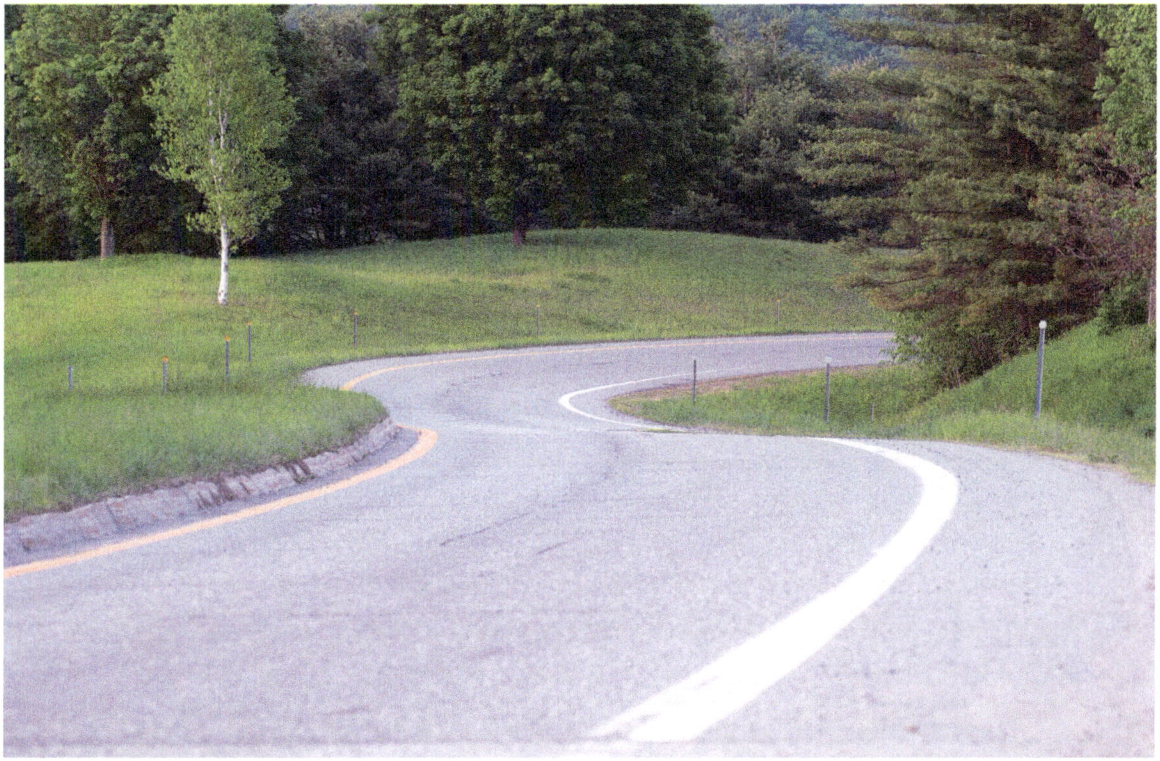

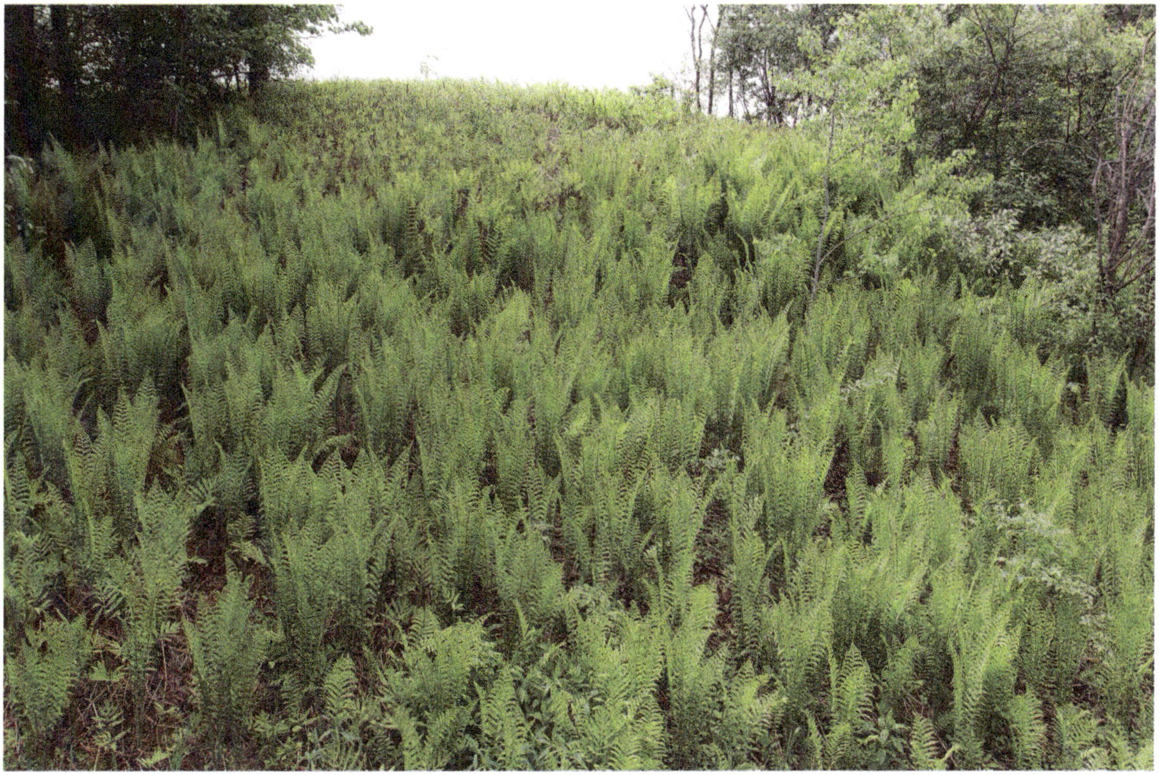

I-89, EXIT 11: RICHMOND (Routes 2, 117)

May 20, 1:00-2:00 p.m. Clouds, rain

Vermont's first governor, Thomas Chittenden, built a home here.
Now, it's *The Kitchen Table*, a swarm of chefs and servers easing
the "kitchen table" (and the family around it) from our minds.
Mary and I "finalized our divorce" here. All that pain at the end
of passion. What we tried to say. What we said. I can't remember
the food. Clouds hug Camel's Hump, rain glittering on lilies of the
valley, diffusing lilac's deep perfume, washing over the dead
chipmunk squashed in a tire-rutted puddle. Somewhere out there,
above the misty valley, Bart Howe must be walking the woods. Old
college friend, back-to-the-lander, who has been back to the land
now for forty years, still living in a lean-to off-the-grid. Bart Howe,
who felt up my girlfriend one night in a hippie love-fest, all of us
blasted on grass, greased up, hugging in a lump of bodies
on a braided rug. Suddenly, a cry, Carolyn's, as Bart's hands
grasped what wasn't his, wasn't wanted, and whatever free
love meant before that moment shifted in my mind to an axe

in the middle of that man's head. Lots of things have shifted
since. Acid trips to acid rain. Warm bread in a brick oven to
global warming. This exit, last hold-out, resists the big-box strips,
resists the condo complex. Richmond hugs to itself, self-reliant,
resists the pressure to put-out, its roads still rutted and windy,
mountains gnarled and scruffy. But next door to Chittenden's
old homestead, the ground's broken for a Caterpillar show-room.
All that heavy equipment geared to tear up a pasture, a hillside.
Warning: Icing May Occur wherever the granite walls close in,
wherever the water forces a bridge, wherever the frost heaves
up and busts the paving stone. An icy wildness will prevail. I say

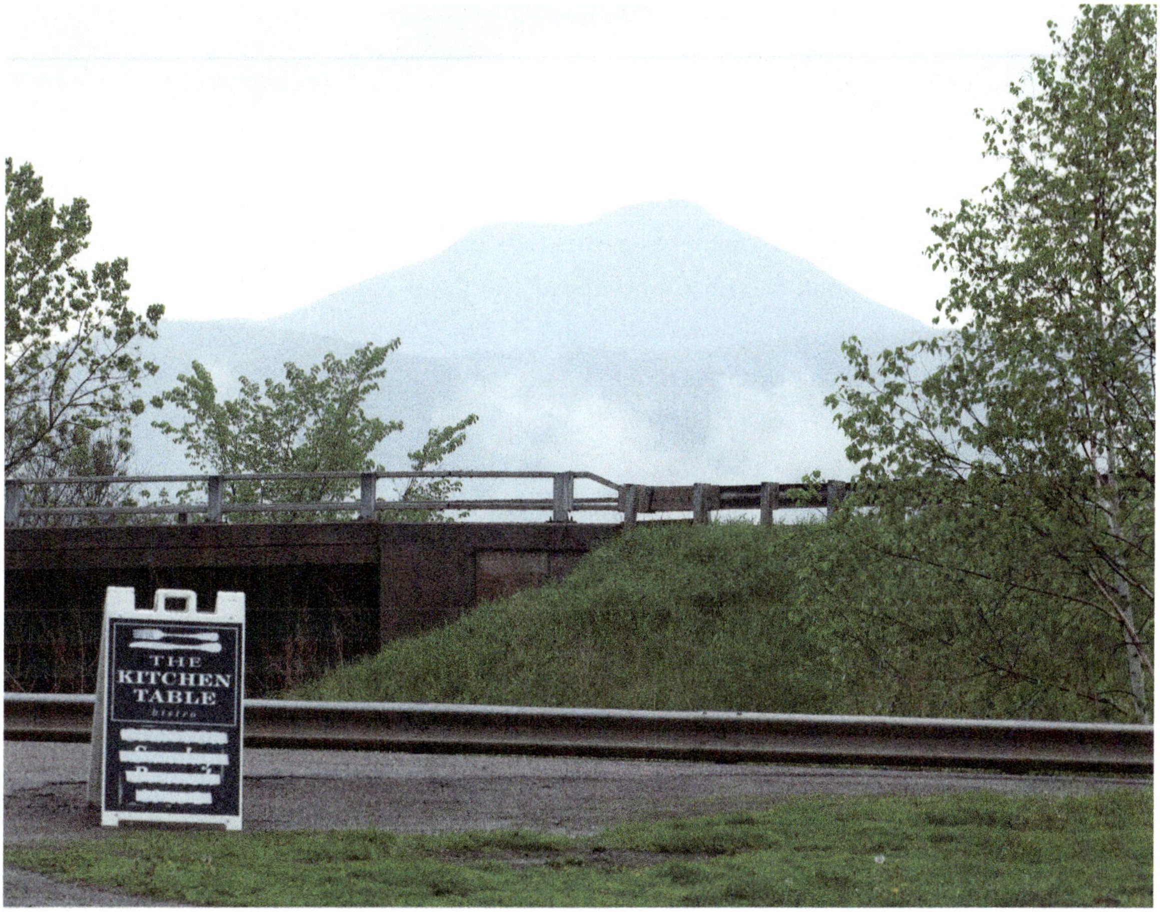

Richmond's an icy diamond, full of facets. "Home of the Round Church," faced 16 ways to Sunday, white clapboard, gold dome, weather-vane pointing in the prevailing direction: *built in 1812, used steadily to rally the spirit and body politic for 160 years*—until, finally, near the end of the counter-culture, it closed forever for repairs.

Someone's Golden Age is someone else's Luddite ways. So the debate goes here. Bart Howe's a throwback. Now, Mobil owns the town's best view, 100 acres preserved by Land Trust, clear-sighted to Camel's Hump.

Now, the Round Church is marked for history, stripped of sovereignty.
Sixteen sides prevent the devil from milling in a corner. (Now he flies
in open air.) The place is a tourist haunt, riddled with pamphlets.
The pulpit's quiet, the pews enclosed, the ceiling vaults buzzing
with wasps. Nearby, a tourist ristorante unfurls awnings cross-street
from the fading pizzeria; chichi bakery floats its smells
into the last Dollar Store. The Winooski swells to flood-stage; *corm
hinds* float up tulips; thunderstorms rumble the horizon, moving
off; clouds thin now toward the top of the sky, promising far-off
brightness for tomorrow. The weather-vane shows wind from the northwest,
Canadian highs coming. Can I build a 16-sided poem? That was our last
supper, Mary's and mine, trying to cover over the obvious pain
with pork chops, potatoes au gratin, Baked Alaska. There: I remember.

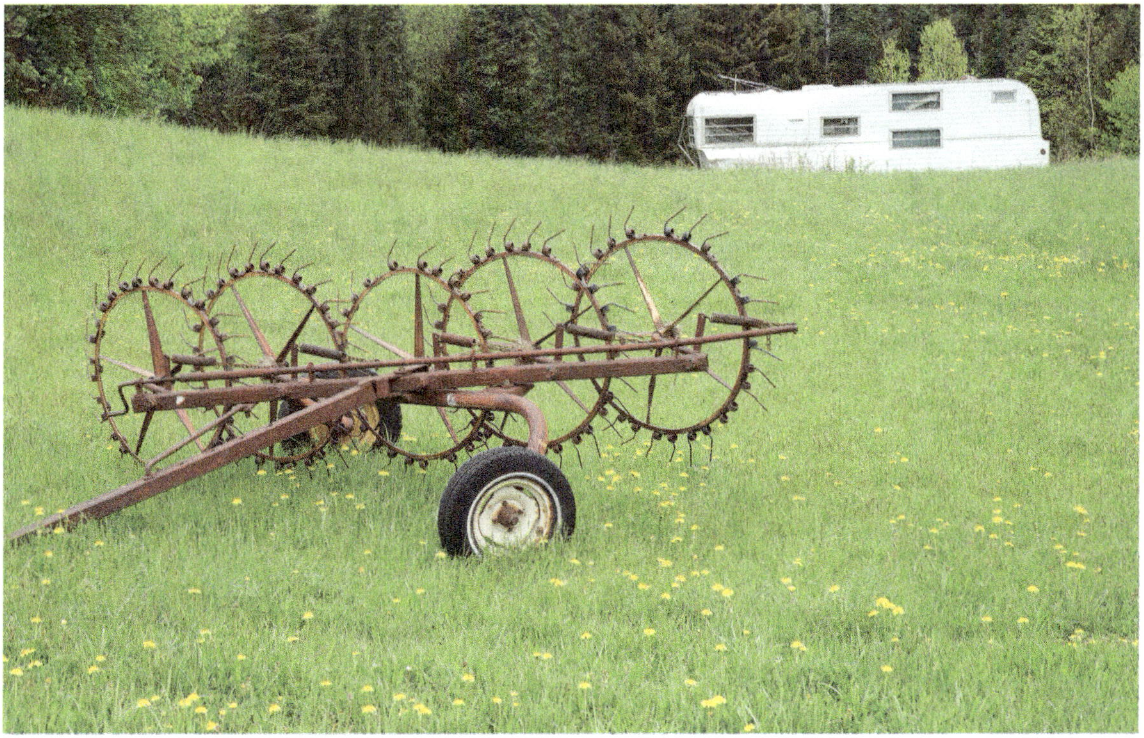

I-89, EXIT 12: WILLISTON (Route 16, Route 2)

May 20, 2:30-3:30 p.m. Sun, rain

Box stores here. Here's a boxy elegy
for what's gone: cow-barn, farmhouse, thousand-
acre dairy. Nearby, talc-mine pond
closed to skinny dippers. State Troopers

complex is a box. Cross-street, what it protects,
WalMart, is a box. Toys R Us is a box,
abbreving a state of being: *Are*:
Existence: the real deal. Not kids

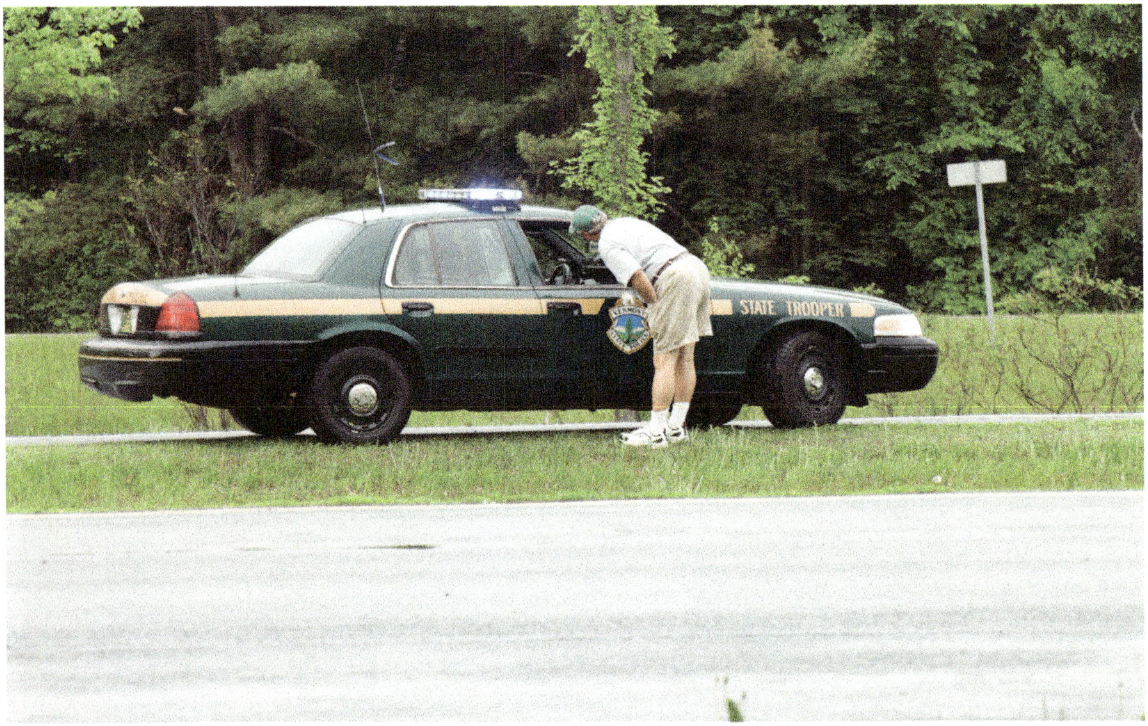

as junior consumers. Bed, Bath and Beyond
is a box. That final word, *beyond*,
once meant something beyond a pillow-
soft world or after-world, beyond

comfort: something terrifying,
awful in its awe, unbidden, un-
bridled, unbound.

Further off, Lake Iroquois. Remember how
its eye opened on black sky's icy stars or blazed
blue in late October's first hard frost? Remember
how those last weeks before the lake froze

you chopped with an axe a swimming hole
for your record year—to swim till Christmas.

Lake Iroquois, where we kissed and skinny-dipped in late October, hollered
hootenanny music, guitar-picking, Jews-harping, Irish-fiddling, claw-hammered
American banjoing, cast-iron pot of chili bubbling on the cast-iron woodstove—
that was Vermont, 1972, before time plucked autumn clean.

Better than any gift

given at a box store, better than owning
a boxy condo, better than ridding
the ridge of Pine Ridge problem-kids. Better
to take the risk, chop circles of ice, plunge
in water, once a day, to scream, alive.

Now, big-box stores and condos are stacked in pastures,
service roads and service roads where not twenty years ago
cows followed nose to tail on muddy paths.

It's that simple: All-Volunteer

Fire Department (gone); Pine Ridge School
for Wayward Youth (gone); Farms (gone), Orchards (gone);
State Police across from box stores (present); traffic lights
and curb cuts (present); sidewalks and Starbucks (present).

Present: stag's head carved on a mausoleum in Williston—
dated 1995—black bear sculpted from a block of wood.

The *town is ill* – animals vanished from the foraging edge
where field meets forest. The living—*I still own, I still won*—

overrule the dead. *See what we have become*.

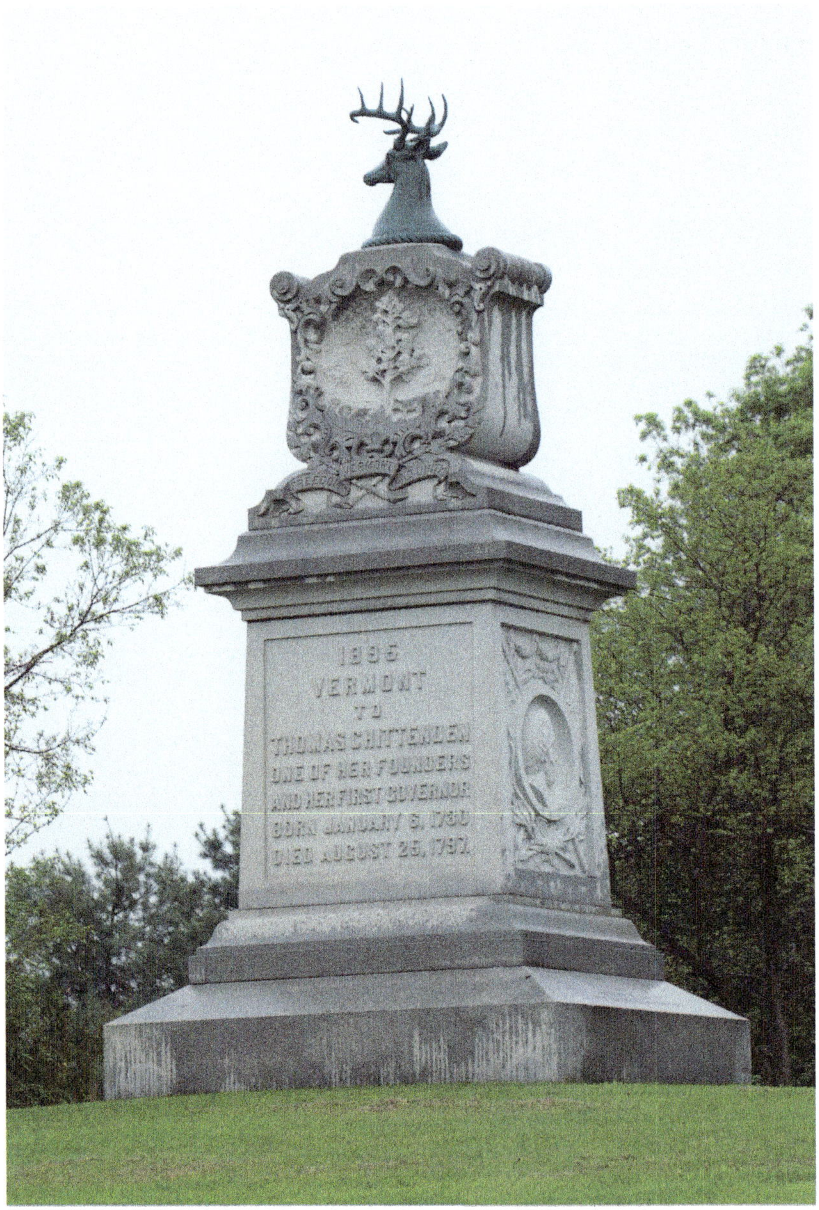

I-89, EXIT 17: COLCHESTER/CHAMPLAIN ISLANDS (Routes 2 and 7)

May 20, 6:00-7:00 p.m. Sun going down

These cloverleafs soaked with spring run-off,
marsh and meadow overrun, land leaking westward,
water drawn down to Lake Champlain: The big river

bulges mud-brown into wetlands so flooded Sand Bar State Park—
its campsites, cook-grills, AV hitches, stone restroom—is underwater,
three feet under, driftwood, dead fish, dolls, and a few floating

buoys, all bumping up against the dikes and sandbags keeping
Route 2 open, from mainland to island, open to a corridor
of anglers riding westward toward their appointment with

fishing rigs casting long lines out to whatever will be tricked
by a spinner on a hook or will struggle with desire to tear open
its mouth, fly off the hook, or die trying. And charity is a bell

ringing in the supper hour, the weekly church fish-fry. Charity is a melody
in a bird's throat at sunset, laughter of woodpeckers, last chatter of
mallards before nightfall—Now, the wheel wobbles untrue, untrue,

flattening in twilight. And charity is a spare that will spare us the night broken down.

John, former side-judge of South Hero, former commissioner of Fish & Wildlife, loved to stock
the lake, loved to ante up for poker, loved to stack the deck in his favor—
the world is your cow, but you have to do the milking—

and that led, for years, to a fixed business of eel-fishing (with a
Scotch reel) on Lake Champlain, night-trawling with flood-lights for the snaky suckers
worrying the deep. Like any penitent, they'd swim toward the light, let themselves be netted by a

fisherman who claimed the lake for himself (*secret Loch*), the sole boat floating over those waters
in the darkness, shining a light, hauling up eels like dead souls, dredging for snakes
that had evaded the first punishments of God and crawled waterward.

John gathered what he could, preserved what he could (in ice), drove
what he could to the border where America is most porous, going northward, where
someone must have let him pass, passport at the airport for a transport plane to France, where eels

fetched the highest price from those Catholic Parisians and John sat down to meals that seemed
paradisiacal. For a while, his was the hagiography, the story of a man who cleaned
Champlain of eels, a tale involving light and its deceptions.

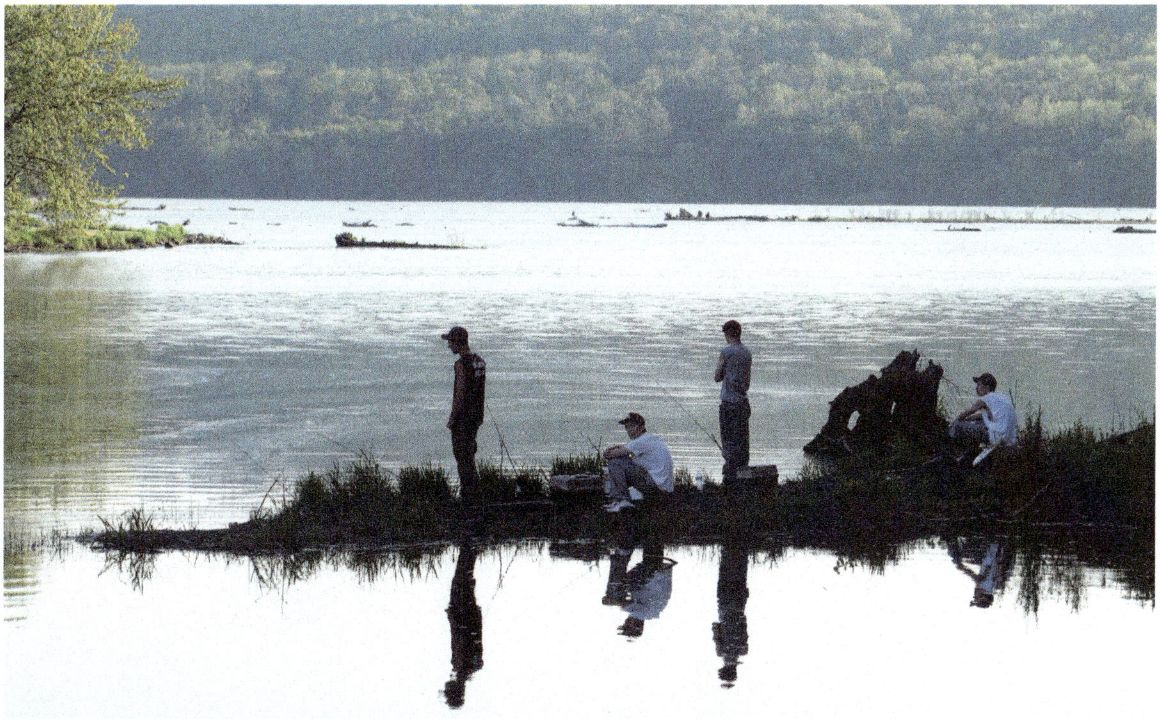

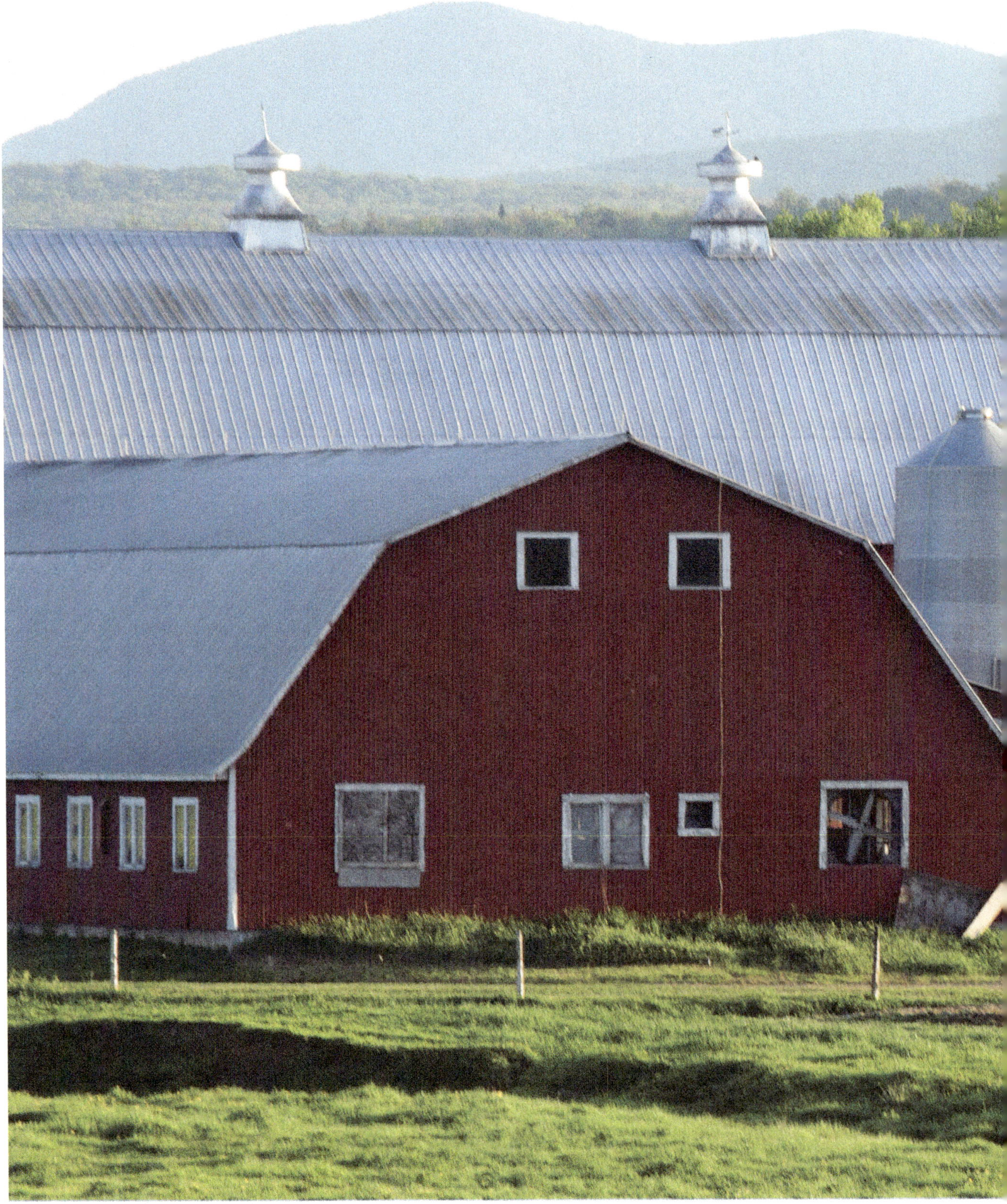

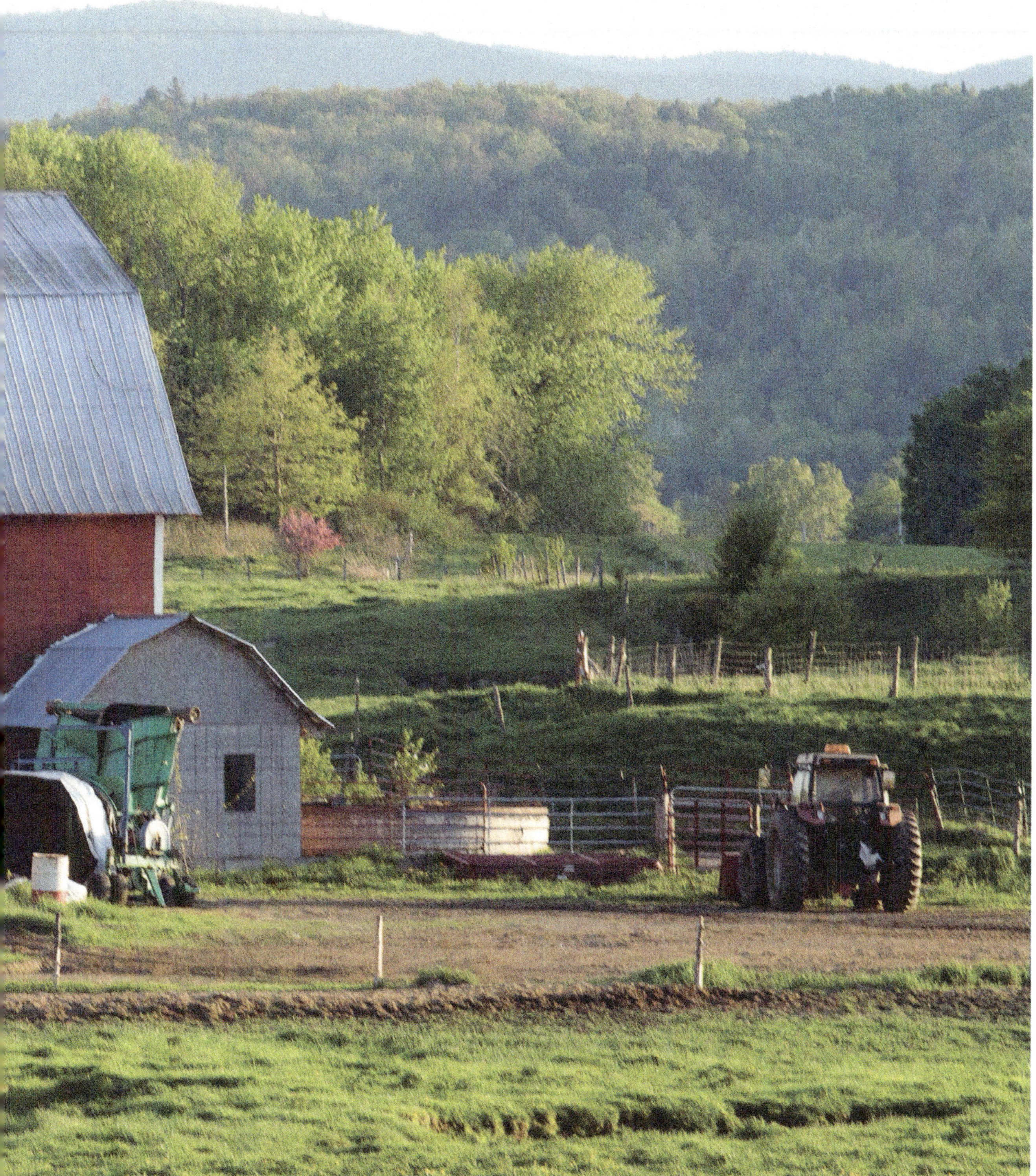

I-89, EXIT 18: FAIRFAX/GEORGIA (Route 7)
May 21, 10:00-11:00 a.m. Full sun

Exit upward toward commuter blue, clouds billowing
in enormous sky. Here, fields open wide, slanting upward
toward antediluvian barns, barn-board and stone leaning, leaning . . .
like a town-planner dozing at his desk, dreaming
of zoning, *a fix far* into the future—tracts of pasture
carved up for mansions, floods of new cash, flush
tax-base, the old barns leaning, leaning

almost off their foundations—*dirty hands*
make clean money—threatening
to take the whole homestead of barn-
swallows, rabbits, foxes, wasps, and mice
tumbling down with them. When they fall,
grander homes will follow. For now,
they lean down as we drive up,

as if to pluck us from our cars and plant us
on a ridge line where a few McMansions
command the view of old Colonials below. *See,*
see? Across the valley, a great white oval—wafer?
water-tower? god? gas-tank?—shadows their lives.
Shad-bloom past. Macs in blossom. Traffic zips along.
Follow it to Georgia Center's eye-blink. A center

with rows of chicken coops can't be downtown, can it?
But there's a general store, computer store—*fax*
a fir!—historical site saying someone, damn it,
lived and died here, and bullied his way

into the town's memory. Edge of town,
the Georgia Freedom Range (golf balls
sailing into a far pasture) tells us what's become

of the town charter—*it makes a difference*
whose cow is in the well—tells more history
of farms to foreclosures than we care to know.
Better to turn up Route 104, upcountry, to Arrowhead Lake,
where the fast-tumbling Lamoille suddenly swirls and pools
over pastures to form one smooth, shimmering evasion for farmers-
turned-fishermen. Here's one place where, when they look down

into their common failure, they see the sky.

I-89, EXIT 19: ST. ALBANS (Route 7)
May 21, 12:00-1:00 p.m. Full sun

Ramp curved as a ram's horn, cornucopia, mile-long feeder
road filled with memories. Cliffs to the east, meadows to the west, and beyond,
Lake Champlain sends a second layer of light into the sky. Close your eyes and look
back. Brenda Corliss shines there. Cult of copper moon-faces she made
for us—call it a *Satan sin lab*, if you want—but it signified nothing
but our bliss of hitching coast-to-coast, blowing dope, bedding down
on sleeping bags, wiping our faces, dinner plates, or tired
asses with the same greasy bandannas.
What's left? *A short pencil is better*
than a long memory any day. Corliss-Blakely, these days, owns a gallery,
a website, an iPhone and iPad paintings: a glowing green pear, a red
pepper sliced open, exposing white ovaries that rise toward a green umbilicus.
What connects us? *Natal basins*. The same three-tiered green fountain in the down-
town park: that day to this, water pours from oxidized copper and assumes
the camber of women: down bottom, the Three Fates snipping threads;
second tier, the vengeful Furies; and on high, almost a no-brainer,
crowning them all, Venus pours and pours her love.

Look back. There was a bar, Tuners, old anarchist joint closed down
by narcs years back. Tuners, where we played honky-tonk piano and chicken-scratch guitar,
where Michael Hurley (Holy Modal Rounder) clambered on-stage with a turbaned-towel,
proclaimed himself Swami Swimmy, and told our futures: every one bound for failure.

Crazy the drug-scene, then, pushing
purple haze, orange sunshine, ecstasy, until someone ratted out every last hippy,
and we pushed on to some other smallville with a sense of play. St. Albans lapsed back

into serious misery, farm foreclosure, lakefront erosion, alcoholics vanished into anonymity . . . among those who left, and later resurfaced . . . Brenda Corliss who I used to kiss and kiss, never serious, just making our mouths into uncontested sites, sharing a drink, a drag, a bath of saliva. Later, her art grew serious— after our hearts had found other attachments, found gravity in love, gravity even in the first floating days of it, because to float required a counter-weight, loaded drug-boats floating on the lake, spirited music at Tuners with a stoned foot-stomping crowd, Corliss and I kissing as the floor shook, the dust rose up.

Spot-light on the funky upright, my fingers cut by the chipped ivories. Strobe-light on the singer, her hips gyrate in slow-mo frames. Black-light on three guitarists whose eyes and smiles are purple-white. Sweat from their shaggy heads shakes into the audience. Applause, then silence. Time works its erasures on Tuners, on teeny-bops, on all of us. That Brenda Corliss has gone missing. This Corliss-Blakely photo-shops her images. It pays the bills. And still, applause.

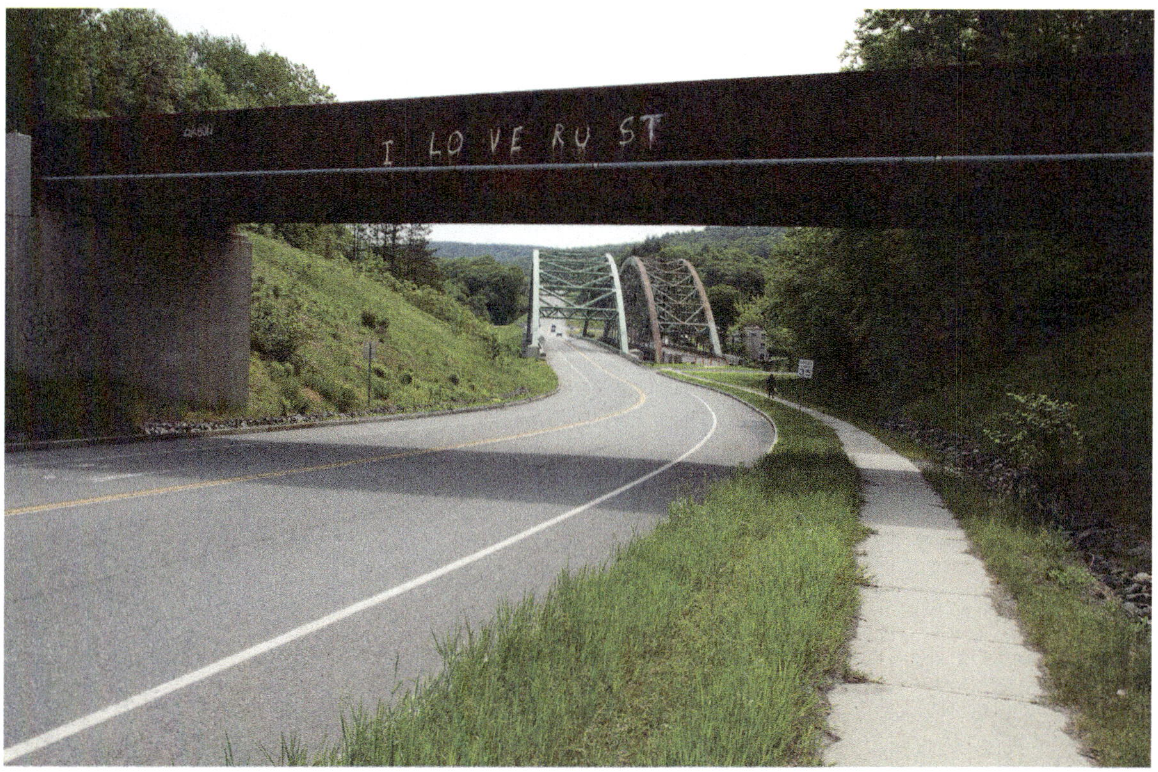

I-89, EXIT 20: ST. ALBANS (Routes 207 to 7)
May 21, 1:00-2:00 p.m. Sun and clouds

Ramp-lands slender as spring
onions, bitter as horse-
radish root. Crowds of blossoms: apple, lilac.
Fingerling trees: ruck of birch, sumac.
Can't tell if they're birthing
or dying out. Signs of wetlands: cattails, cauls
of skunk cabbage, marsh marigold. Surprised
how a slight place, an after-thought, really,
becomes a community—like this after-thought
of an exit, miles north of city center,
skinny feeder road to Canada.

A few big-box stores sprout
amidst cheap real estate, a few shiny franchises:
Cobb Auto; Handy Cadillac. A few things hang on:
St. Albans Drive-In, last outdoor theatre
in Vermont. Ah, the open-air make-out scene
of days past, squawk-box speaker hooked to the door,
convertible top fanned down, bugs biting
whatever wasn't already covered
by groping hands.

Live while you live
and then die and be done with it. Last drive-in with last
movie from last season posted: *Pirates of the Caribbean.*
Heart-attack start to a new summer: triple-header car-
chase thrillers: *Bullitt, French Connection, Vanishing Point.*
Squawk-box speakers gone, now just tune
the radio to a local frequency, and voila. Cinema!

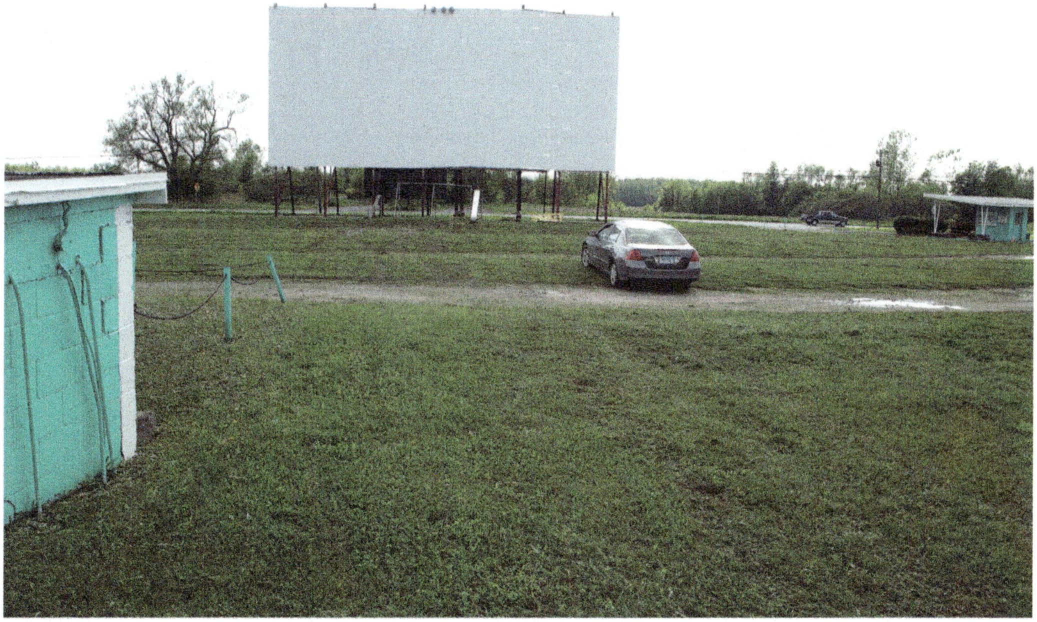

Almost died here on an icy Nor'easter night in '85,
fiddling with the radio, speeding along a feeder road
until the abrupt STOP sign popped red in my headlights,
braked too late, skidded at 60 straight across the highway,
plowed, impossibly, between cottonwoods, into a pasture,
miraculously unharmed, except—

today that pasture's vanished. Now, crowds of trees
stand where an open field stood a quarter-century past.
If I had today the same foolishness in me, to drive devil-
may-care in a blizzard, I'd have hit that maze of woods and died—

Part of me damns time for changing the scenery.
Part thanks the fates that bygones are bygone.
Cheer the new Energizer Battery factory across from Advance Auto Parts.
Cheer Price Chopper and Blockbuster, the spiffy Yoga Centre.
Cheer them presently, while further down the road,
mourn the farm sold in foreclosure; the Esso sign: Gas 29¢;
mourn Second Hand Rose: Clothes by the boxful. One Buck.

I-89, EXIT 21: SWANTON (Routes 7, 78)
May 21, 2:30-3:30 p.m. Full sun

TWO SIDES OF THE INDIAN NICKEL:
HEADS I WIN, TAILS YOU LOSE

Sweet, sweet town. Could raise a family,
if it weren't for them *wantons*, them Indians
raisin' Cain. Swanton's got a piece of Champlain,
sparklin' on its backside. But them Indians
claim it's theirs for the fishin'. Damn Abenaki.

I 'member back to 1980, the great Fish-in Trial. Indian-give
was what it was. Said they was *indigenous* to these waters.
Throwin' round words like *aboriginal* and *slaughter.*
Damn albinos is what they are,
not a one of 'em dark enough to cry native.

Then the damn campaign: license plates sayin'
Abenaki Nation. Missisquoi Tribe. They can kiss
my royal backside. See how they like to suss
out my two butt-white license plates. Cuss
'em, they can have the back-end

of Swanton, down by the worn-down four-
story hotel, just 3 letters: TEL.
Where'd the HO go? Laughed all
the way to the bank like these bald-
faced Abenaki fakes. Let the bank teller

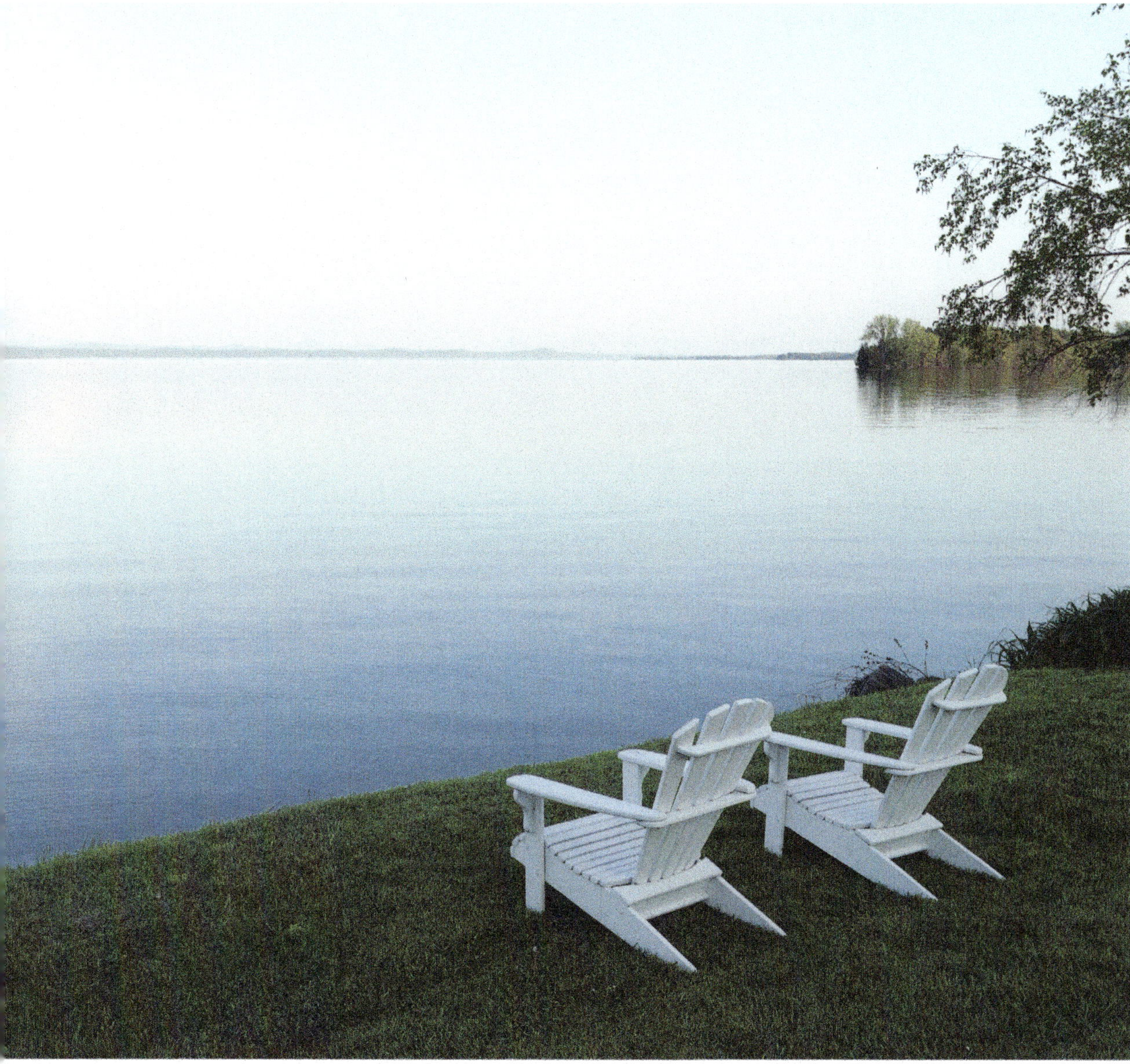

tell 'em: No. He *wants no* free fishin'. Buy a license
like every white somebody.
Judge Wolchick be damned, givin' fish away
for free! So the sheriff and his deputies
took custody of the case,

thank you, brothers and sisters,
very much. Harassed every damn Abenaki squatter's
license plate with a red rising sun and wavy blue water
stamped on it, impounded the cars,
made those suckers walk like their ancestors.

Next, they was cryin' foul 'bout some hidden
agenda: some Eugenics survey, they say.
Targeted for extinction by white society.
Cranks and crazies, that's who the Abenaki
are. Too much liquor, weed and women.

Sweet, sweet town. Gazebo on the green,
Christian rock band crooning *Thank you Jesus.*
Smitty's Starter & Alternator by the river.
Hotel closed. Just 3 letters left hanging.
What's "TEL" w/out the "HO"? (I don't know.)
Bob Shakow bought a sprawling Victorian

for a song right there on Maple Street.
Bought up the neighborhood, really,
it being the '60s, notified his buddies,
land's cheap, and these "refugees

from the cities," as they called themselves,
showed up, chipped in, and bought

themselves the sweetest neighborhood
on the northern shores of Champlain.
Couldn't complain; it was a sweet deal.
But the Abenaki claimed it was a steal.
Shakow and his gang were so decent
they sold it back to them

for a smart profit, then moved back
to the land, it being the '60s, lived in teepees,
lean-tos, even a long-house or two, whooped it up
like Indians, and some of Shakow's gang
slept out under the stars, sang protest songs
amidst the plenty of pot, booze and women.

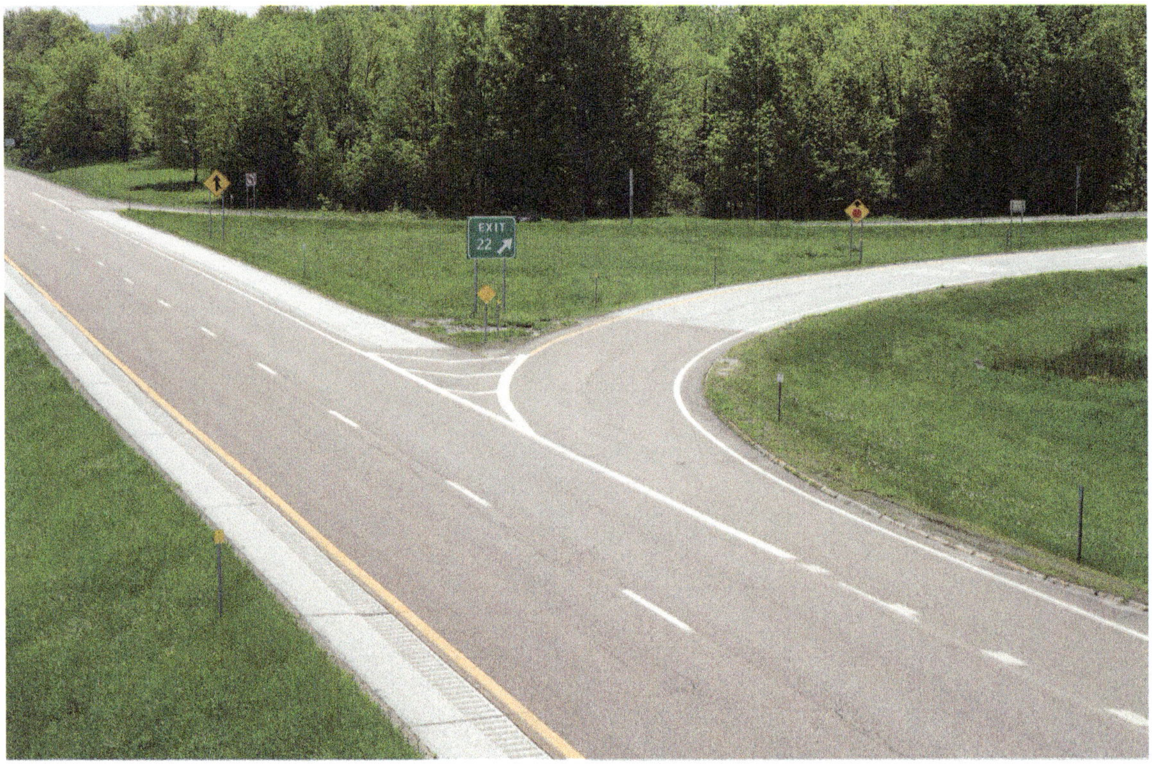
EXIT
22

I-89, EXIT 22: HIGHGATE (Route 7, End of the road)
May 21, 4:00-5:00 p.m. Sun and clouds
"Border Ahead"

America ends here, chirr of a blackbird.
Route 7 turns to marsh and pasture.
Ahead, there's serious scrutiny, border
guards asking your what and wherefore.

You have to hoe a row of corn with a man
to know him. If you're coming into the country,
tough questions snap you to attention.
Eat a peck of salt with a man before

you trust him. On Border View Road,
there's a Vet in a wheelchair looking glum
in the sun, there's a large American
on a sit-down mower trimming his view

of the border. If you're leaving the country,
there's a friendly *Bienvenue*, a backwind
easing you through the desultory A & Q.
Love thy neighbour by pulling down the hedge.

This border's porous by nature, sings the hermit
thrush, hundreds of miles of deep woods and wetlands
unfenced, unpatrolled, balsam fir and blue spruce
so thick they'd do what? Stop a masked invader?

sings the cedar waxwing. Or a slinking belly-
crawling border-crosser? cries the river otter.

Cross over to croissants and the Cri de Coeur,
cross where the Anglicans and Quebecois

wrangle the language bilingual. Cross
where Hessian conscripts once fought for the Brits,
later, lost the war, lost the border,
wandered into Highgate to work the mills,

grind axe and scythe, or ride milled logs downstream
to Lake Champlain. In Derby Line, today, I've heard
readers enter the library's front door in America
and revolve through the rear door into Canada.

The power of books overcomes the small-
mindedness of borders. Little emblems—
US Customs patch of stars and stripes—
pose questions so precise the musing mind

slips through. Little epaulettes on wings
wing across whatever borders are, following flyways
more ancient and important. Sky-rivers full
of birds wind their great migrations northward.

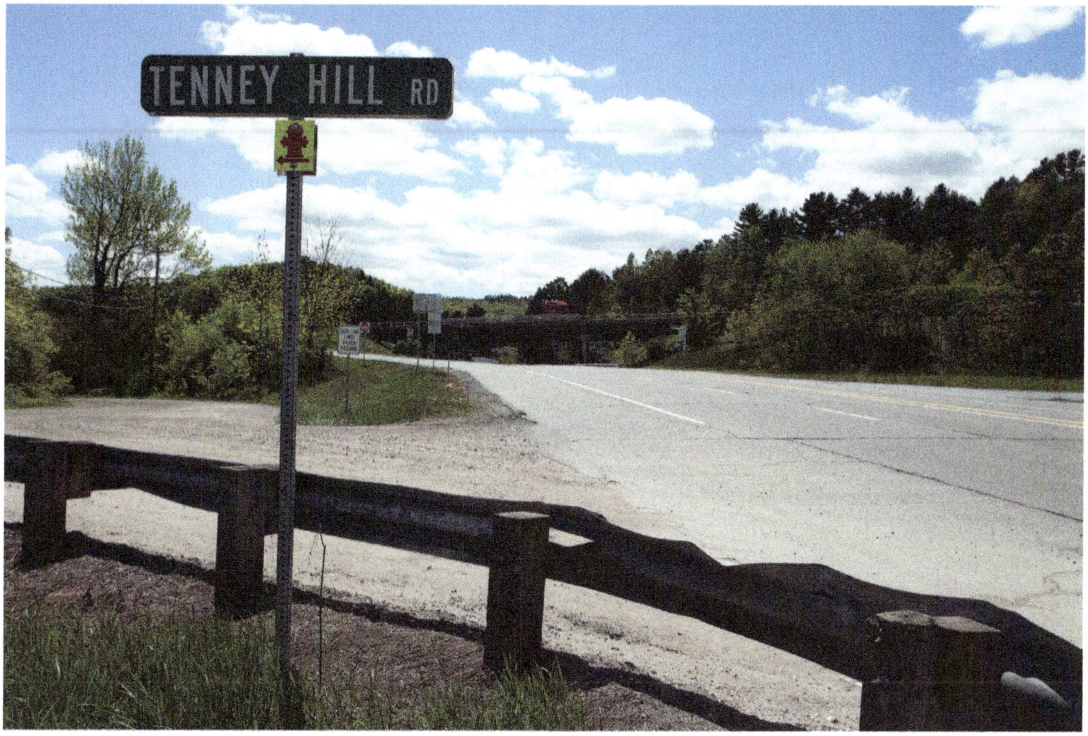

ROMAINE TENNEY

May 17, 2:00 p.m. Full sun, cumulus clouds

Hello, black fly. Thanks for the welcome.
Now I know what Romaine Tenney cursed
and loved here on Tenney Hill Road: the sting
inside blossoming, the black bother
at the center of the eye bent on spring beauty.
Tenney knew what was coming, and it came:
the interstate that brought the commerce in,
and with it, the quick-buck with its quick-
made and quick-fading values. It didn't
value Tenney's enterprise on a hill farm
that was collapsing around him. He lived
in the mudroom ell of his old family home

with gingerbread eaves and wrap-around porches
sagging, lawns and meadows stretching
in all directions. In the mudroom he was
closer to his animals: 30 milking cows,
20 laying hens, two teams of workhorses,
some sows, some goats, and four herding dogs.
He lived for them and for himself as days
folded into days and he daily tilled the soil
or tinkered with machines that made the farm
hum. He ate simple: oatmeal, biscuits, beans.
He drank switchel or spring water. He watched
over his fields. He watched the workers up-
valley gouge the land to make the inter-
state. He studied a document: Eminent
Domain. He said: No to the 10 thousand
they offered, No to the 13 thousand
simoleons they said were his last chance.
He said, No value you can place on this
place that birthed me and gave me my daily
bread, my milk and eggs, my purpose on earth.
I ain't leavin'. You'll have to throw me off.
And that's how the sheriff found him
when he came with his men on a Friday
in September to empty the house
and the barns. Tenney was gentle as always,
sadly smiling, eyes pooled blue as he watched
the dismantling of whatever it was
to have an estate seized by the state.
Yes, Tenney knew what was coming, and it came:
the highway, that is, whizzing by beyond
this Park & Ride where I stand today shaded

by a "Tenney maple" (says the plaque) rooted
roughly in the middle of his farm, rooted
two hundred years ago when his grand-kin
settled in. Tenney might have wince-smiled
at "Wally's Road," extending from the Park
& Ride with a sign "Private Property—
No Entrance!" Tenney tried that once:
private property. Little good it did
with government bent on progress. It was
progress and plain misfortune when
a surveyor with the gouging road crew
at the end of a long day laying road
and right before sunset saw sun glint
off the weathervane on Tenney's barn
as he squinted down-valley for the way
forward, and said: *We'll site the road there,*
straight through the middle of that man's farm.
Yes, this must have been a sweet piece of land
back then. Now it's a four-lane with a median:
cars going south would have driven straight
through his cow-barn. North-bound traffic
would have run him over in his iron bed.
Now the place is nothing . . . or the saddest spot
in Vermont, where a man lived sixty years
before he burned it up, burned it down.
He loved it all, the land, the animals,
the husbandry. Never married, he wedded
the fields and woodlots. The land was his,
and he was the land's. And time had nothing,
and everything, to do with it: Time
in which generations could pass without

the least change to road or rail-bed; time
to talk across a roadway, lawn, or orchard
of apple-blossoms to kith and kin or tourists
from the cities to the south who sought
"a real Vermonter," lanky, bearded, wry,
with a gentle light in his eyes, a light
content with his self-made life, and only
himself to praise or blame for a problem
and a cure: in 1964 the highway came
straight through his home, the sheriff came
to move him off the farm, and sometime
after midnight in his 64th year,
Tenney set loose his animals, set
the farm on fire, trudged back to his bed
and closed the door on autumn, bolted it,
spiked it shut, loaded his shotgun, and
triggered it as the house smoked and blazed.
Self-immolation was his only protest.
The hillside burned for a night and a day.
Afterwards, the road crew worked
in a stupor. The surveyor drank. And the state—
the state—never tendered a note of
condolence to his next of kin (never
mind an apology). They just progressed.

He was born there. He loved the land. He loved farming. He loved—I'm talking truly loved. He worked hard every day, seven days a week, and it was all out of love—not out of duty or commitment or need. It was the love of the land. That's all it was.

—Rosemary Tenney, *sister*

I-91, EXIT 12: WILDER (Route 5)

May 22, 2:45 p.m. Sun, clouds

Wilder! Granite pass, state troopers flash
blue strobes. Don't get pulled over. Dash
down a slick incline, maple and pine
in a green cloverleaf screening you
from the trooper's view. Slide into
a turn towards town, two hitchhikers
in green shirts going the other way: Woodstock,
White River, somewhere hitchhikers are still
hitched to. Play with the radio. On a ridge
above town, radio towers, cell towers, air
full of wavelengths and microwaves. Wave
at the kids on ten-speeds. Wave at the lawn
keepers hedging bets and sod at Sterling Springs,
"a planned community" of scoff-laws and law-
abiders, as the day demands. Second homes
or salaried posts close to Dartmouth. Radio
says, Sale on graduation flowers. Hotels
and B&Bs filled. Other digs? Saint Anthony's
Cemetery on Route 5 has room for more
O'Neills, Schettinos, and Lakowskis. Blood's
Catering Service (steaks and seafood)
is hiring part-time. And the Charles F. Wilder
Community Center offers its usual largesse.
Behind the pumpkin clapboards and leaded
glass, the one and the many make their pacts.
It's a working class town by the looks of it
(and looks can be transparent) with a new
bloom on the rose: pot-holed roads that rattled

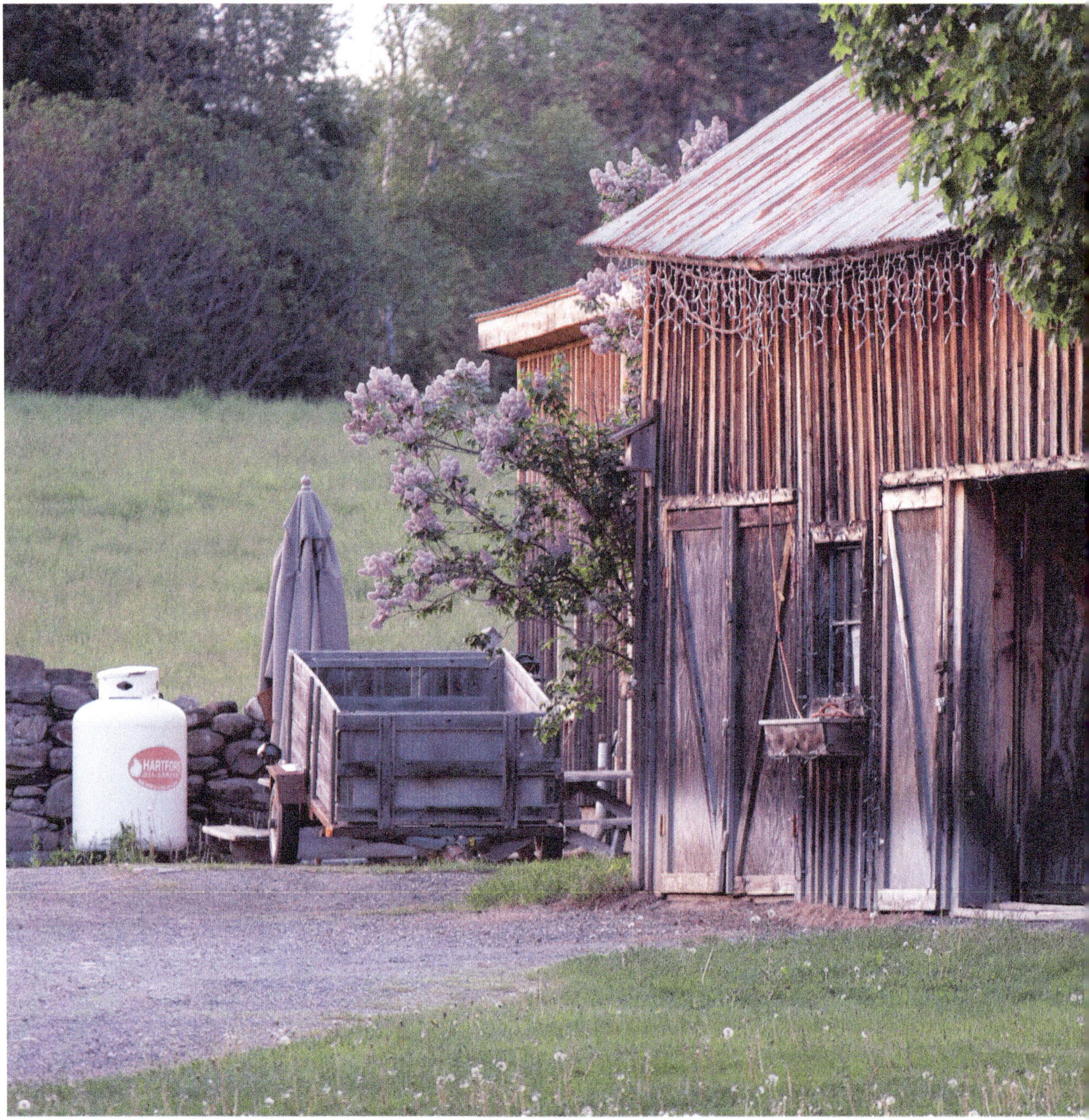
HARTFORD

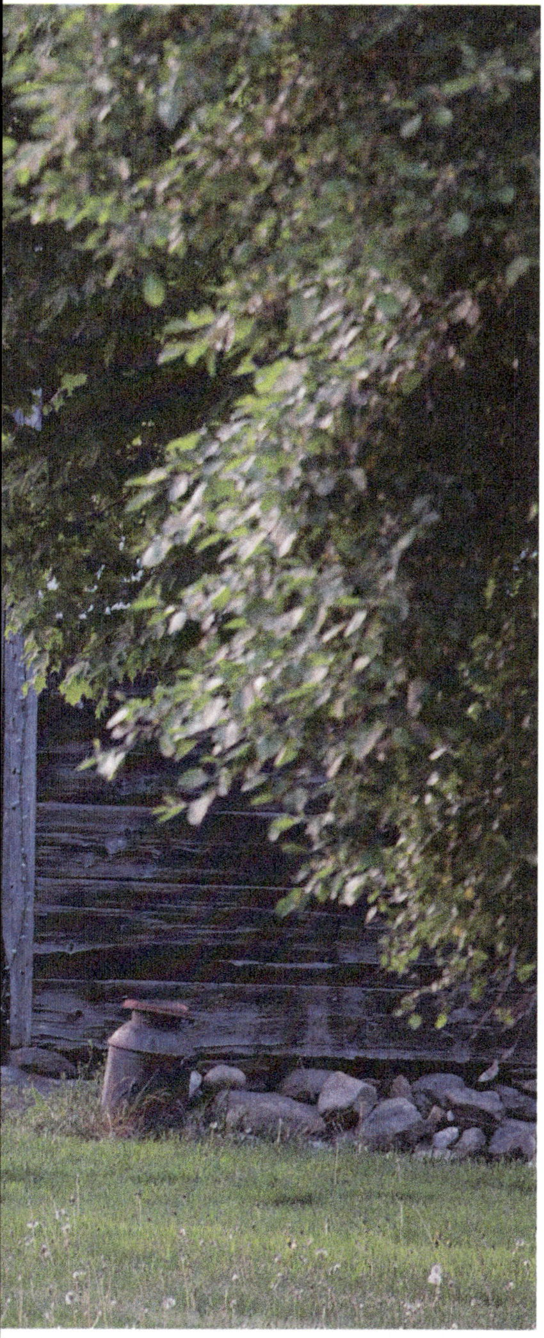

the window-glass are filled, porches that hug
the roads are double-braced, and sidewalks
that were painted lines in tarmac slowly
rise as concrete forms. All say what they say.
A man sprays weed-killer on his lawn.
Another hammers a For Sale sign. Up
and down the road lilacs waft and flash
their purple clusters. Slate roofs shine.
You can smell the dam beyond the town.
It smells of spring and promises in the making.
Mortarboards and gowns are just a town away.
The real estate's revived. Great neighborhoods.
Great smells. The town hall's pitch is perfect:
Just wild about Wilder!

I-91, EXIT 13: NORWICH (Route 5 VT; 10A NH)
May 22, 3:30 p.m. Clouds, sun

Such a thin slice of ramp-land
for such a thick slice of the pie
in these apple-blooming towns,
Norwich and Hanover.

Once you're in, doors open.
Take the handsome bridge over the river
toward an old enlightenment:
magisterial, symmetrical, reasoned

by town-fathers in town halls,
8 enormous concrete balls (faux Classical)
decorative on the marble bridge (like
doorknobs opening secret passages

to Hanover [admission, for instance,
which everyone knows is class conscious]).
Waterside, a park with Adirondack chairs
(chained to concrete blocks), and picnic

tables made in Coventry, RI, by
Seaside Casual Furniture Company.
Yellow warblers flit in the lilacs.
Kingbirds dip their tails and shit on tables.

This is the Founder's site: log huts
for the Hutchinson and Messenger
clans who first wintered here in 1765.

Can you see them? 250 years ago,
hacking with axes the hardwoods and the soft,
scooping up mud from the river, reeds from

the banks, patching it together against winter
after winter . . . already staking
their claims. Today

we have our ample homes
and our homeless. 250 years hence, time
availeth not (as Whitman says). We see you, future
denizens of Norwich and Hanover, in a density

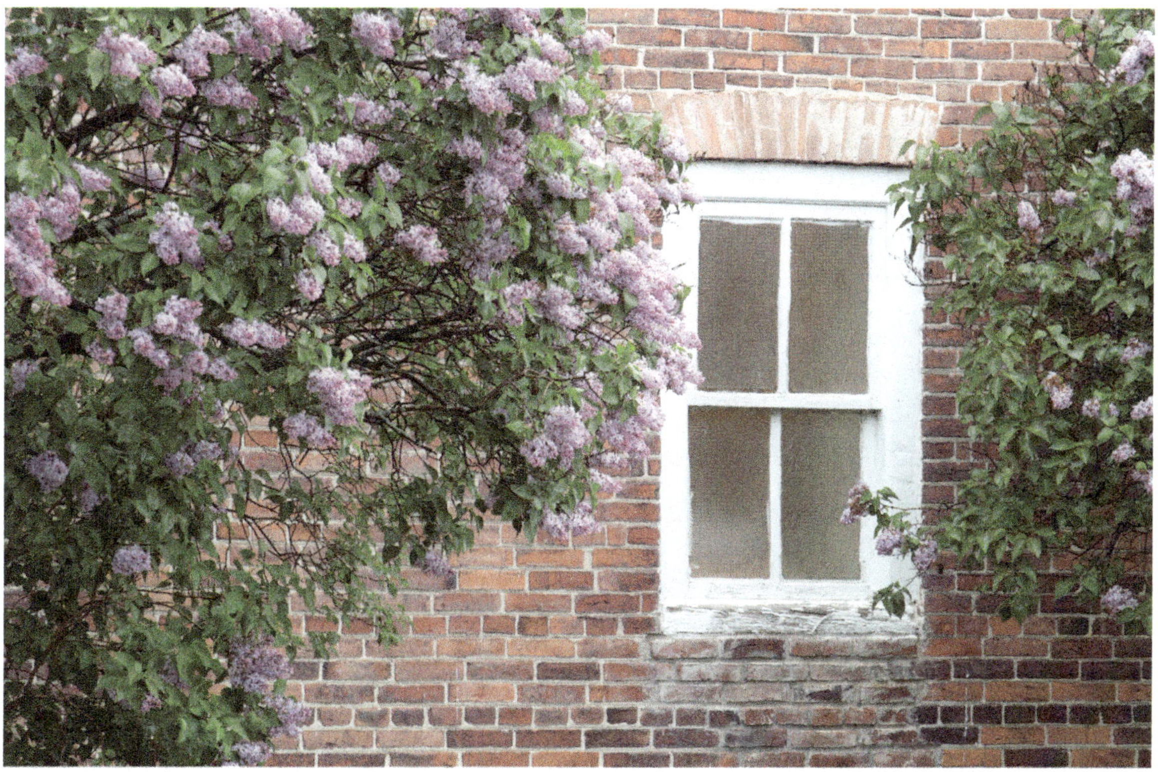

of development along the river, pulling
back and pulling back as the planet warms
and redefines the flood plain. Time
availeth not, future citizens! Just as I

worried my mind was over-mastered
by the elements, so too will you worry.
Just as I felt the gray matter surrender
to reason and another dozen levees,

so too will you worry. Just as I surrendered
to commerce backed by science that would
save us from ourselves while our dreams
withered under the increasingly punishing sky,

so too shall you worry. Just as I questioned
the teleology of ornamental things and answered,
Because we can afford to, so too shall you question
and answer. Just as I marvelled at blackbirds nesting

wherever they could, on a ruined river barge,
on a highway bridge beam, repurposing
human structure into nature, so too shall you marvel.
Just as I smelled lilacs and apple-blossoms

on a spring day, so too shall you inhale them
and name them First Things Owned
By No One. Lilac is nature's answer
to human insufficiency. So shall you find it.

I-91, EXIT 14: THETFORD (Routes 5, 13)
May 22, 5:00 p.m. Sun, clouds

Lit vistas on the highway between Norwich and Thetford.
Plenty of room for cumulus-glow and mind-lit memory to play
this life against another. Nature's first gold in the trees, chartreuse
pastures, dandelions zoned liminal against marsh marigold,
our car climbs toward hillsides flooded with sun. Her hair was gold,
her gold wire-rims, her gold fillings glinting in a laughing mouth.
Dilapidated cabin off a 4th-class road, a leaf-covered path,
a piano out-of-tune in one room, a sagging double-bed
in the other, but what gold tones it hummed in the Thetford heat.
North of White River, exits expand in leisurely cloverleafs.
More land, more leisure. For instance, Thetford Academy's
handsome holdings on nearby Thetford Hill, a small village
of stately colonials, edged by equestrian zones,
gentlemen's farms, and two boys' teams on the playing fields,
kicking soccer balls, tossing softballs. I never played with
her kids. Funny the things a marriage sheds. The boys
stayed with their father. And we wandered the midnight
trails to find glow-worms' phosphorescence, hoot
owl's call, a sudden rush of wings in a moonless night
right before us. Nearby, Grace Paley made a second home,
a long way from Brooklyn. I can hear her accent in the woods.
I can hear the cadence of her prose. I can see her laughing eyes,
her mess of white hair, her jaw always chewing something,
sometimes just an idea or an injustice, which the forest knew
nothing of. But she knew it and brought it here. And the forest
had to listen. Just as she had to listen to the forest. I'm confused
by vistas that let in too much light. My mind can't make sense
of more than a few perspectives. I wish I could multi-task

like my daughter who comes out of the shower singing
a new pop song and announces she loves existentialism,
finds baseball boring, boys exciting, has a yeast infection, and
she's writing a paper on code-switching among the urban Wolof.
Can I even get this all into a poem? The clouds are moving fast.
And Grace is gone from Thetford, from Brooklyn, from anywhere
I can name, but her name is on the cover of City Lights
publication No. 6, just one beat book after Ginsberg's *Howl.*
And I imagine her lighting up the sky just now as she crosses
toward her next destination. And that woman I mentioned
in lines 5–9 is long gone from my life. I don't know if she's
walking with Grace or with her grown kids or with a new man.
I hope she never returned to her husband. That story was over
before I arrived at I-89, Exit 1, or I-91, Exit 14, or any
of the other exits that were my entrance to a sun-lit column
of time through the blasted granite where we laughed together
and parted, finally, because of time (our mismatched ages)
and another flash of gold that turned my head to other
opportunities. What a convenient evasion: "opportunities."
Sorry about that. East Thetford is ruined by Route 5.
Trucks rumble by outside the trembling houses.
Further afield, on hillsides, along the lakes, the land's
dearer, the habitations trimmed and ornamented. I never
traveled to Thetford Center, five winding miles off highway,
but I bet the light glows there on a town with a "real" town
center, a village green fenced with split birch, and lilacs
purpling late daylight. I just bet it. And Grace and
that woman I found before the time of fireflies,
when the ground was still pregnant with glow-worms,
are there, too. That's how vistas work. That's what we imagine.

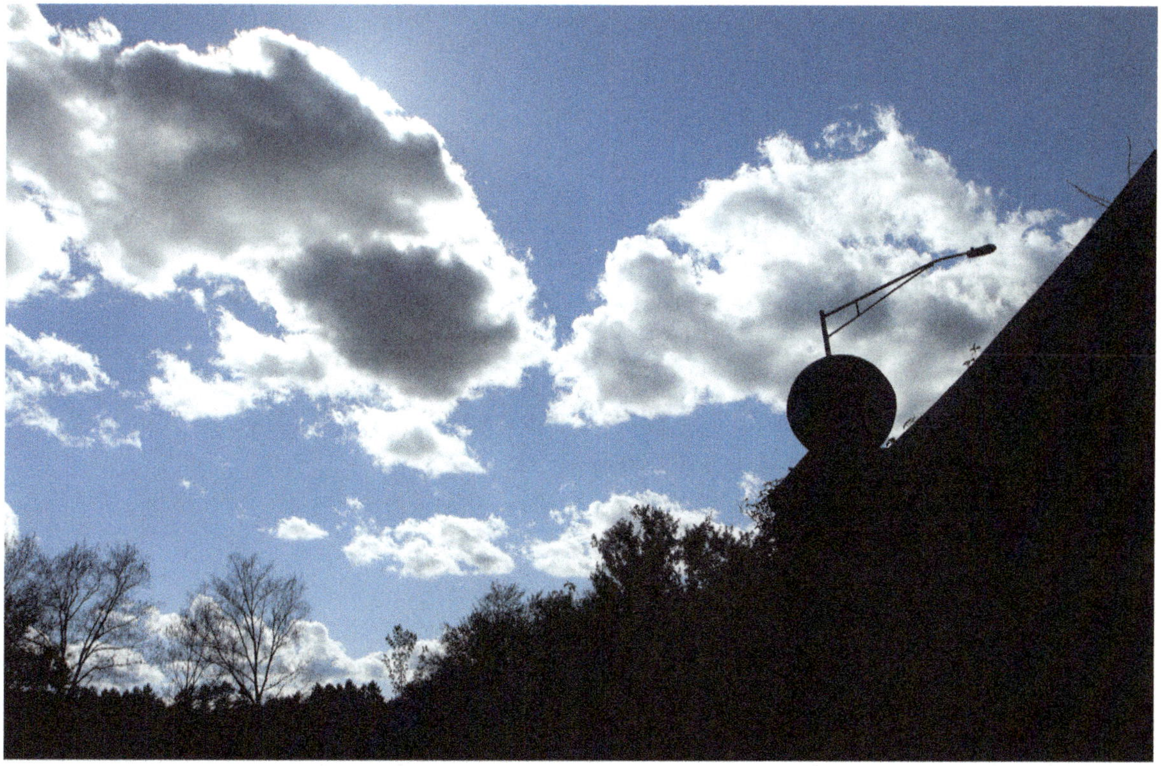

I-91, EXIT 15: FAIRLEE (Route 5)
May 22, 5:30 p.m. Sun, wind
"Lake Morey, Lake Fairlee, this exit"

Equivocal exit, granite scarp, apple and lilac
blossoms soften the stone. Lake Morey
sparkles off the ramp, chop in the water,
wind from an Arctic high, a few white sails
diagonal in the distance. Today, remoteness
reigns—maple and beech bend to tamarack
and spruce, light seems to glance off polar
ice, high and cold and isolate.

On a *leafier* day, lake tamed, the mood
would be carnivalesque, the richer
residents across the river in Orford, New Hampshire,
would spill from their whitewashed mansions
to golf along the lake or take the plunge.
Anglers would load up at Country Boys
Bait Shop and stop at Joey's Scoops or
Whistlestop Café, and all would follow

the sign: *Buckle Up, Your Friends Need You.*

Now, remoteness reigns. Lake cottages closed.
The lake, a cool, inhospitable blue.
Golf greens gone blond and missing
their pins. Hulbert Outdoor Center,
with faux-chateau and lavish cabins,
boarded up. Only here and there,
smoke from a winterized home
beside a stylish gambrel barn.

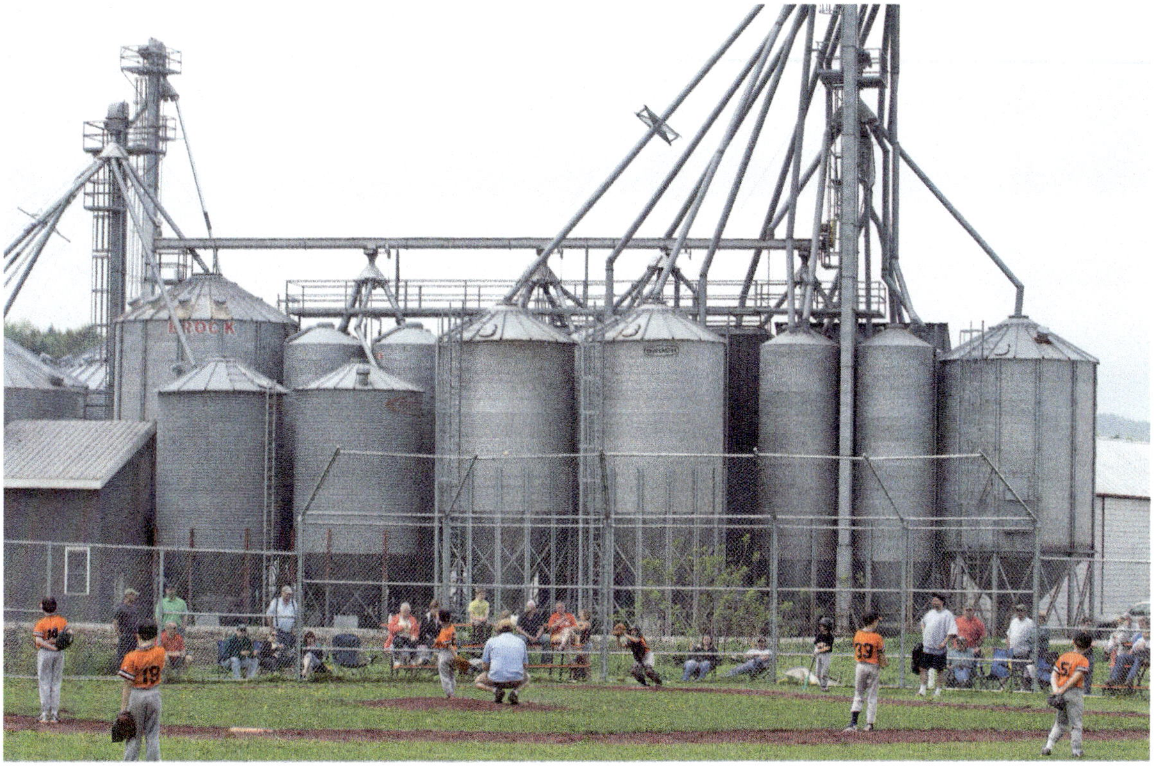

Drive to Fairlee town, where Route 5
makes a mess of neighborliness.
Not idly will you cross over
the four-lane to banter with a neighbor.
Stop at Community Paints for the unvarnished
truth: *You only treasure what you can't possess.*
Stop at Fairlee Feed & Saddlery for the down
and dirty: *Sometimes even love shows a re-run.*

Stop, for sure, at Whippi Dip Snack Bar,
the varsity baseball team lined up and
yammering for ice-cream on a cool afternoon.
"Soft cones are for dorks," says the rangy right-hander,

holding a hard cone in his mitt and chomping it.
"Soft cones are for lefties, and lovers," says
the smaller teen, giving his Creemee a swirling lick.
"Here's to southpaws," says the service-girl, winking

and handing him another covered in jimmies.

Nearby, a young mother lets her toddler explore
the piano on the patio; he plunks a rhythmic pattern
as he wobbles back and forth from bass
to treble clef. Even on this finger-numbing day,
all follow the sign on the painted upright:
This instrument lives outdoors for your playing
pleasure. Play it, if you have an ounce of talent.
Play it if you can make your neighbors dance or sing.

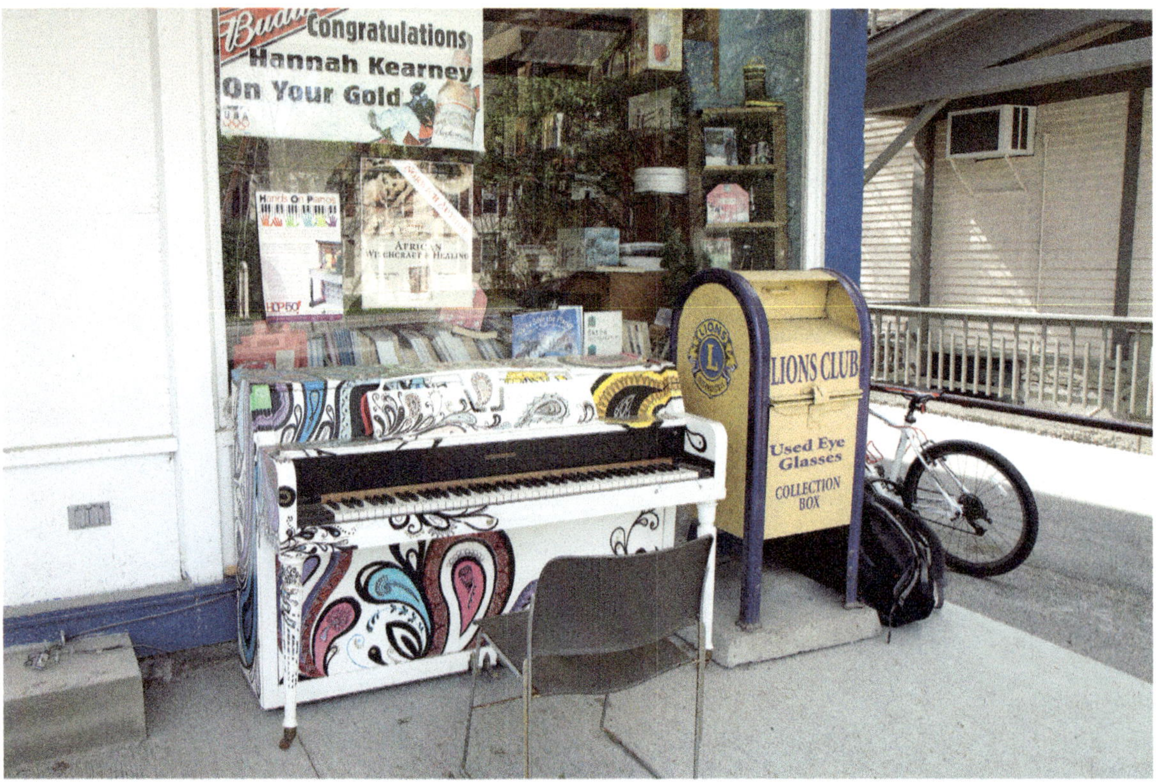

I-91, EXIT 16: BRADFORD (Route 25 to 5)

May 22, 6:30 p.m. Sun, clouds

"Home of James Wilson, first American globe maker"

Down-sloping ramp with scraggly pines
opens onto meadows with wide views
of the Whites. North Woods Café ("a smile
a mile wide in every scoop") and Hungry Bear
Bar & Grill, with lots of local talk
in the parking lot ("Long winter. New
truck? Or just got it cleaned?"
"Cleaned it. *Drab Ford.* Took a winter
of salt and mud off her. Big news here—
got a litter of pups. They'll eat us clean,
if we don't sell 'em. Want one?"
"Nope, bank already owns me.").

Drive forward to the Bradford strip:
Mr. Puttz Miniature Golf (sounds like a bad
Jewish joke in the Borscht Belt) beside
U-Store-It (selling Slick's Ice Cream) beside
the Connecticut River Academy ("teaching
the relationship between what you learn
in the classroom and how it's used
in everyday life"—James Wilson's
spinning in his grave) beside
the A.E. Hale Funeral Home &
Self-Storage Unit, this mix of
businesses trying to make it
in the Northeast Kingdom.

Drive downtown for the brave facelift:
Millwaters Tavern, Colatina Trattoria,
and specialty coffee, The Local Buzz.
In order to discover who you are, first learn
who everybody else is. You're what's left.
Downscale seems to pull with equal weight:
lots of shops, founded on dreams, now closed,
and old dependables—Hill's five-and-dime
and Perry's Oil Service—still persevering.

Still, folks need to marry and make
the next struggling generation.
Today, a hundred cars park on Main
for the Methodist wedding. Stately
Colonials on both sides of a wide avenue
say something once happened here:
foundry and machine shop, two gristmills,
three sawmills, and whetstone factory
crowded along Waits River. James
Wilson designed and manufactured
America's first globes, molding
theory to practice. Folks finally knew
where they were on earth.

Today, Old Church Community Theater features
Cookin' with Gus, playing through June,
cross-street from Bradford Academy
that long ago taught the liberal arts
(both *where* we are on earth, and *why*)
and long ago closed its door,
repurposed for a global
economy that's bound
to shrink the world.

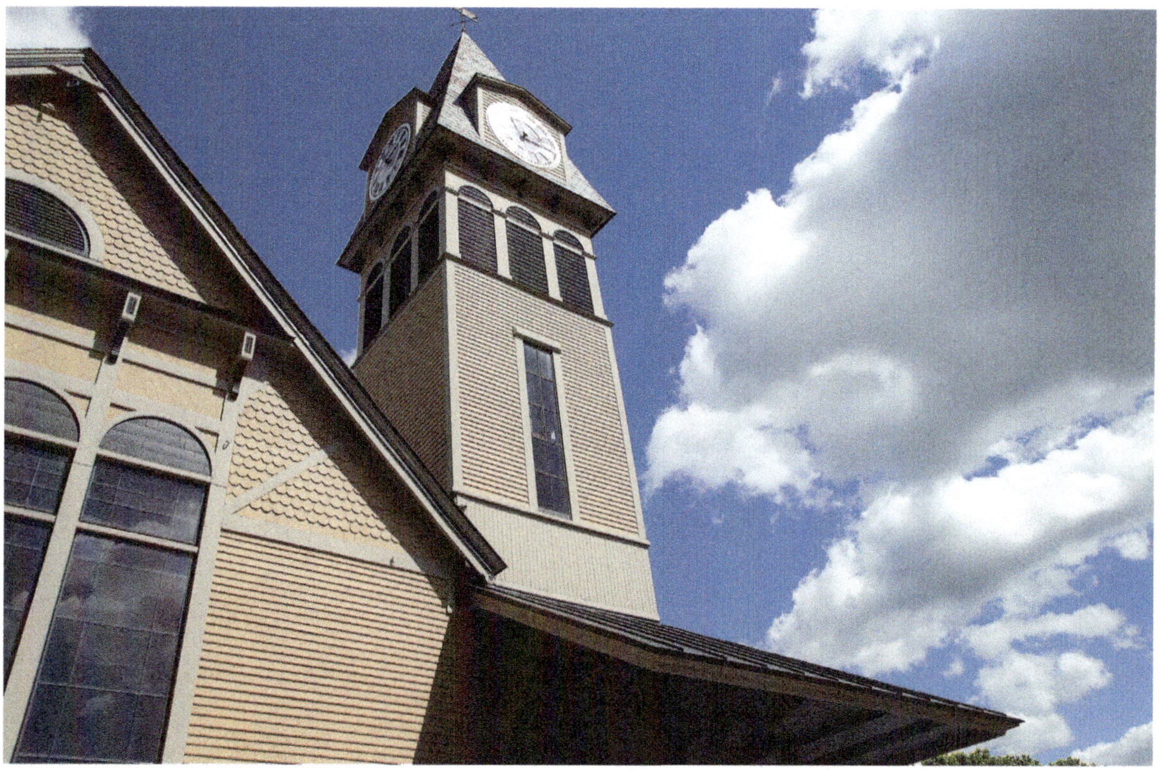

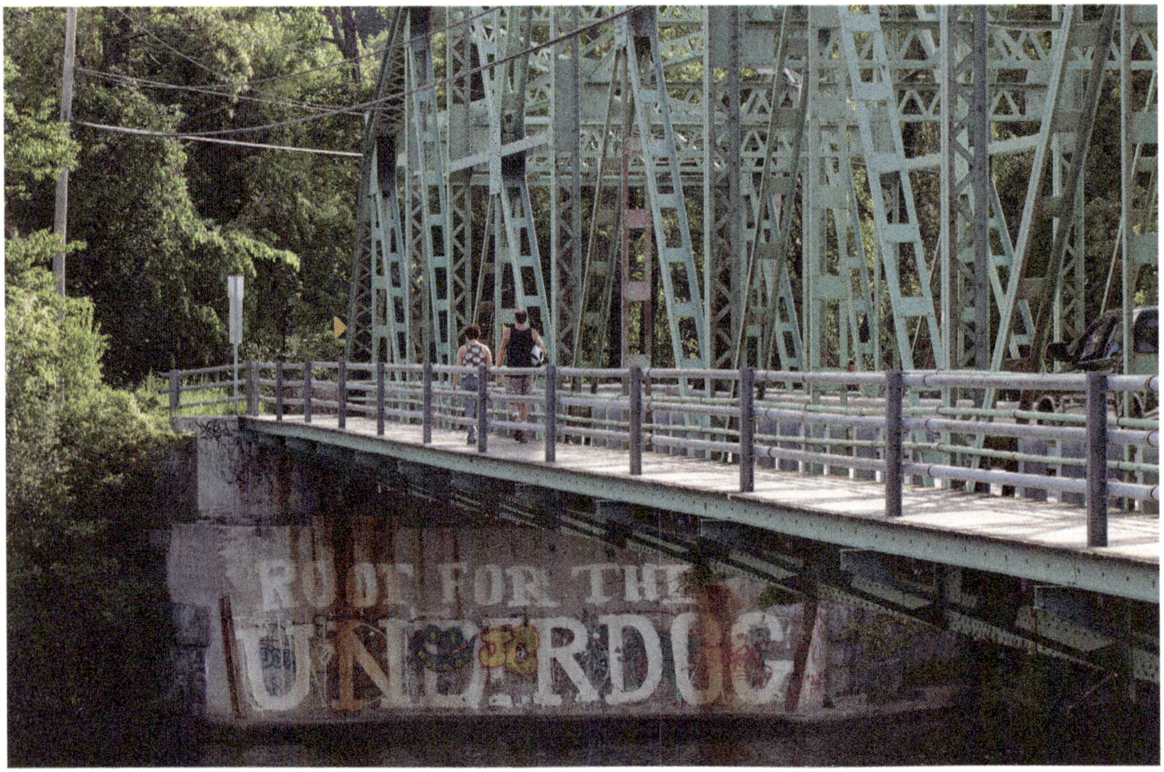
ROOT FOR THE
UNDERDOG

I-91, EXIT 17: WELLS RIVER (Routes 5, 302)
May 22, 7:00 p.m. Late sunlight

Apple and crabapple blossoms ablaze at sunset.
Roll down the ramp to P & H Truckstop and color
it local for the 300-pounders on the diner stools,
the Yankee pot roast, turkey and cranberry,
"genuine, serious sinker donuts," and the world's
best maple cream pie. *Outside you'll smell*
diesel but inside the warmth and waft
of homemade bread. You'll see
the cook with the braided beard,
the waitress with patriotic hair,
you'll hear *Radar Love* on the jukebox
and truckers weighing in from everywhere.
Boltonville cemetery's just a stone's throw.
Must have been a town here once,
now just the dead dusting their stones,
three miles upwind of Wells
River. Wells River swirled
with business in its time. Now,
it's caught in an eddy, pulled down
to #254 (of 282 Vermont towns)
on the *livability index.*
Some folks try to raise it up
with Rising Spirit Yoga, Dragonfly
Den Massage, Yankee Scents, Solar
Solutions. They don't drive uphill
to P & H Truckstop; they walk or bike
to Bread & Chocolate Co-op. Vice versa
for the loggers and truckers whose pick-ups hum

up the steep incline to P & H and swear
by its maple-cream pie. They want
better than minimum wage and no damn
tampering with the culture. Moot point
in 1808. You'd have seen canal boats
guided by long poles floating downriver
laden with lumber, clapboards and shingles,
returning upstream with iron, salt, and rum.
"A relatively crude settlement,
hamlet of 10 buildings, without
schoolhouse, church, store, or
professional man of any sort."
Careful what you wish for.
Coosuck House served the 1800s
traveler well until it burned. Replaced
in 1900 by Hale's Tavern, Italianate
hotel, which served for 50 years until
it crumbled. Replaced, in turn, by *a service*
station, the stage stop of modern travelers.
Now, high on a hillside, out of town,
there's another station, P & H,
posting the numbers: *Mean*
per capita income in Wells River:
$14,000. Come in and eat all you can!

I-91, EXIT 18: BARNET (Route 5)
May 23, 10:30-2:30 p.m. Full sun

Hoover flipped a switch in Washington
in 1930 and the Barnet dam
opened its sluice gates to let the waters
flow—cold Connecticut waters,
backed upriver seven miles, pooled
a mile wide, a hundred feet deep—
and water has moved
the body and the mind in Barnet
ever since: white-bearded, white-haired, pony-
tailed farmer spills off his porch
and says it's only May but already
the farms need rain. Next door, a man
in mechanic's overalls hoses down his mower.
Beyond's the Barnet General Store,
with a stream and waterfall flush
against its foundation, with signs
and portents and auto-parts and prayer-
flags and flyers for Buddhist talks
at Karme Choling. These days,
says the town librarian, folks get their news
from spirit-groups, three sects residing here,
all with hundreds of acres and prayer halls
and acolytes from away. Barnet's a town
of conflicting flags and faiths:
on the mechanic's porch a blue flag flaps—
United States Marine Corps. Nearby,
the yellow flying tiger of Karme Choling;
Milarepa's banners of red, yellow, and blue;

another with red, white, and blue (American);
another and another. They're all flapping
in a breeze filled with lilac and apple blossom.
They co-exist on this high hillside with a high vibe.
That's why the Buddhists settled here, they say.
Whatever wasn't high then is high now:
a black butterfly alights on dandelions
and, within an hour, turns yellow!
Through the town center tumbles the water.
Next door, *Samadhi Cushions* for the meditative
mind that cares about its postures and comforts.
Inside, cushions, robes, incense. Outside, blossoms
scattering across the lawns. Contemplative drift.
Lilies of the valley open their pale bells
in the library garden, and I kneel down
to sniff their sweetness amidst the mulch.
The librarian kneels beside me, says,
Those bells are pretty, but poisonous.
Says, *You've seen this town, now see*
Karme Choling. Best way to know
the two sides of what we've got here.
And so I go. Instead of the vacant grounds
I'd imagined, I find a hundred cars
in the lot, license plates from 30 states,
and not a human sound. Just wind
riffling the trees, blackbird's *conk-la-ree*,
and phoebe's wheezy repeat.
At the flagship building, two entrances,
one with a red carpet flowing down stairs;
I trudge up until I hear a scream: *Get off the carpet!*
That's for His Holiness! I settle on the porch

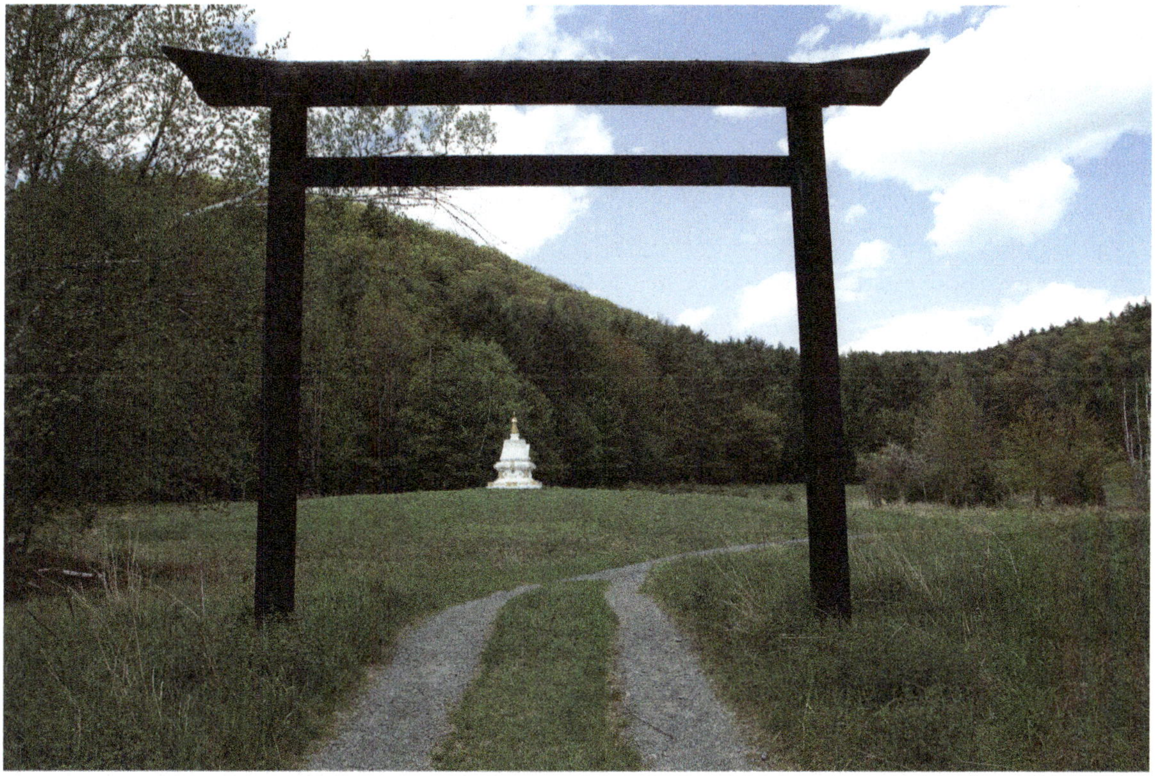

and listen to the breeze, then stretch and stroll
the dirt road. But an acolyte in tan khakis
and red beret (paramilitary!) trots toward me:
Get off the road! His Eminence is coming!
Back on the porch I go. The acolyte
instructs: *Trungpa's eldest son is here:*
Sakyong Mipham Rinpoche. He has taken
the place of his dearly departed father.
He is coming down the road. When you see him,
you must stand and bow. A black limo accelerates
toward us, skids to a stop, swirls dust.
Three bodyguards spring out. One opens
an umbrella, and His Eminence emerges
in robes and sashes, wearing slick sunglasses.
I'm wearing shorts. He sees me, smiles, and bows.
He whistles up at the blackbirds, and they whistle
back. He tilts aside the umbrella and lets sun splash
his face. He flips a tiny switch in consciousness
that floods the mind. I bow. His Eminence ascends
the red carpet (my sole-smudges visible) and enters
the main house. Then, a hundred acolytes rush up
for lunch and the unpacking of his lecture.
For me, there's a long walk up a hillside
to the stupa where ten years past, Trungpa's body burned
on a funeral pyre. Hawks circled above his floating ashes
and a double-rainbow arced the sky. Now spring blossoms
surround me in this meadow cirque and many
streams trickle and shine on the musing mind.

I-91, EXIT 19: LINK TO I-93 (Littleton, NH)
May 23, 3:30 p.m. Blue skies

Nothing but a link to Littleton, a brighter state
of nature—the Whites' high peaks, snowmelt's
glistening trickle, clear brook or river
over quartz and granite; mica sparkle
across a moraine; kettle pond undistorted
for ten fathoms—but a more benighted human
nature if *Live Free or Die* leads to the NRA, Loeb's
Manchester Leader, and Dartmouth's
mouthpiece, *The Reactionary Rag*.

O, leave it be. Enjoy the long roadway to nowhere
but commodious vistas inviting whatever spirit
is, in its ineluctable, irreducible state, to gaze
through undefiled eyes of a May morning
before it's clouded with cant or commerce
that turns a clear day to haze.

(O, keep us from desperation, so hot
to touch the transcendental we'd rip
through metal rails and fly off the road!
O, link us to the living, for all its fitful seeing.)

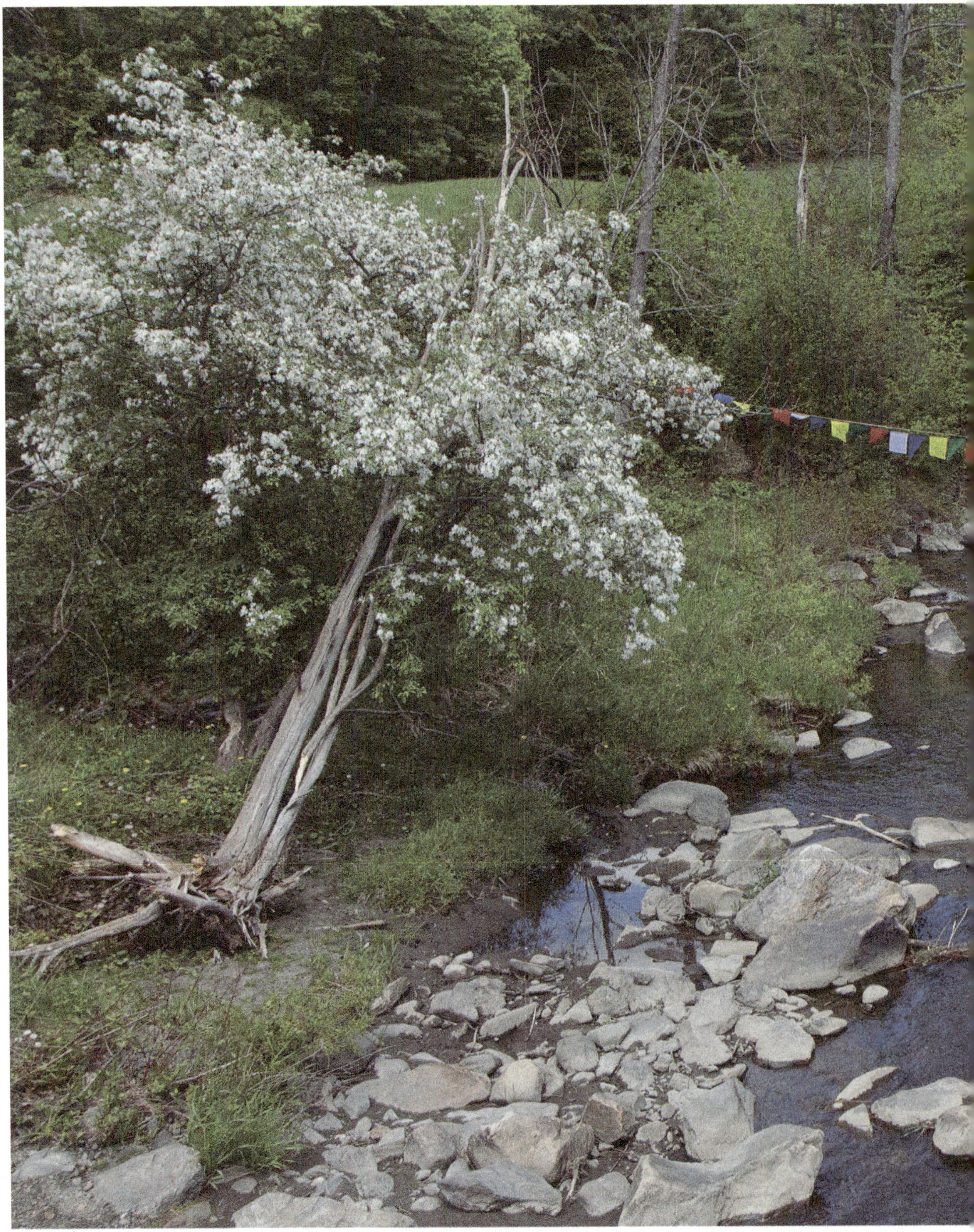

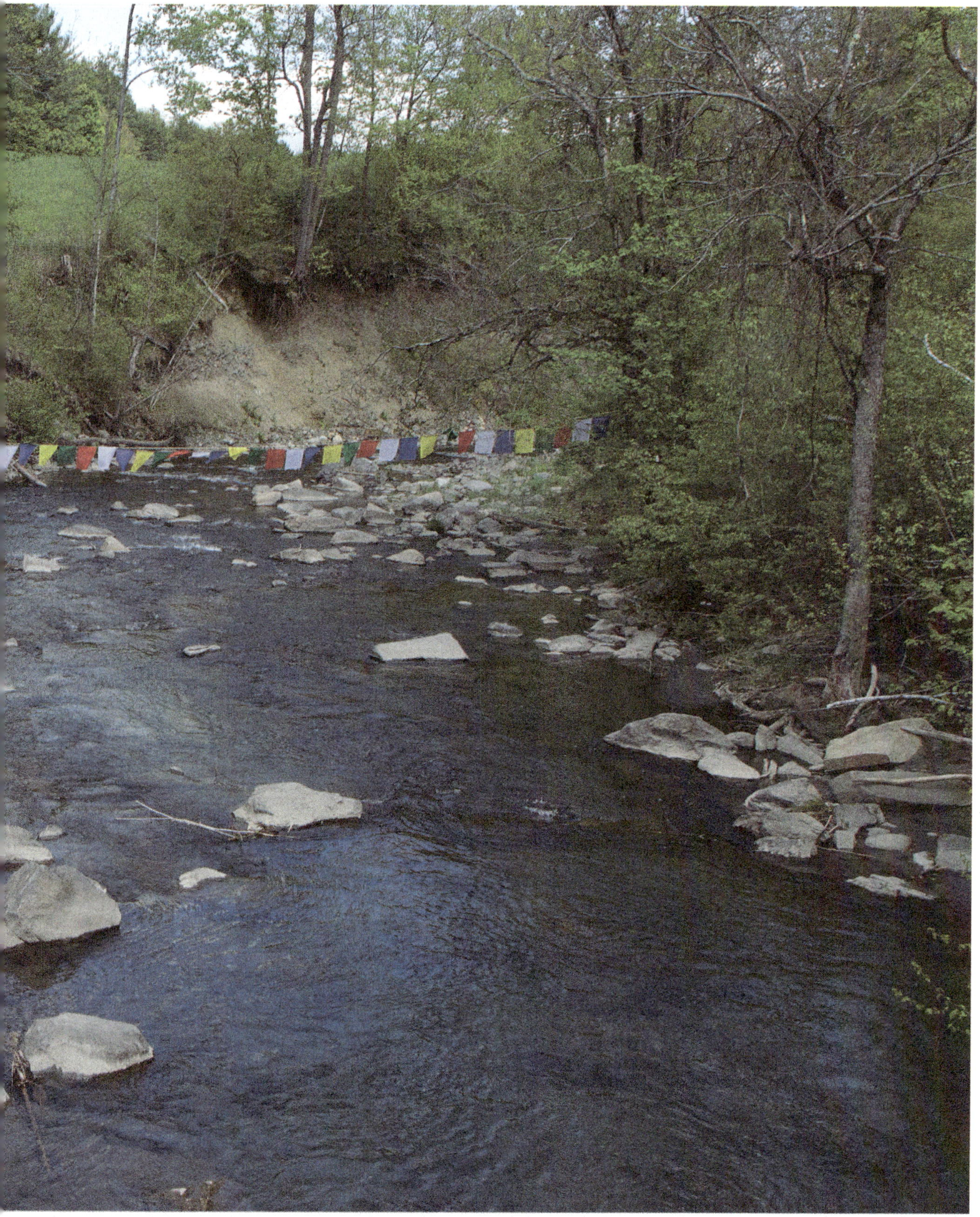

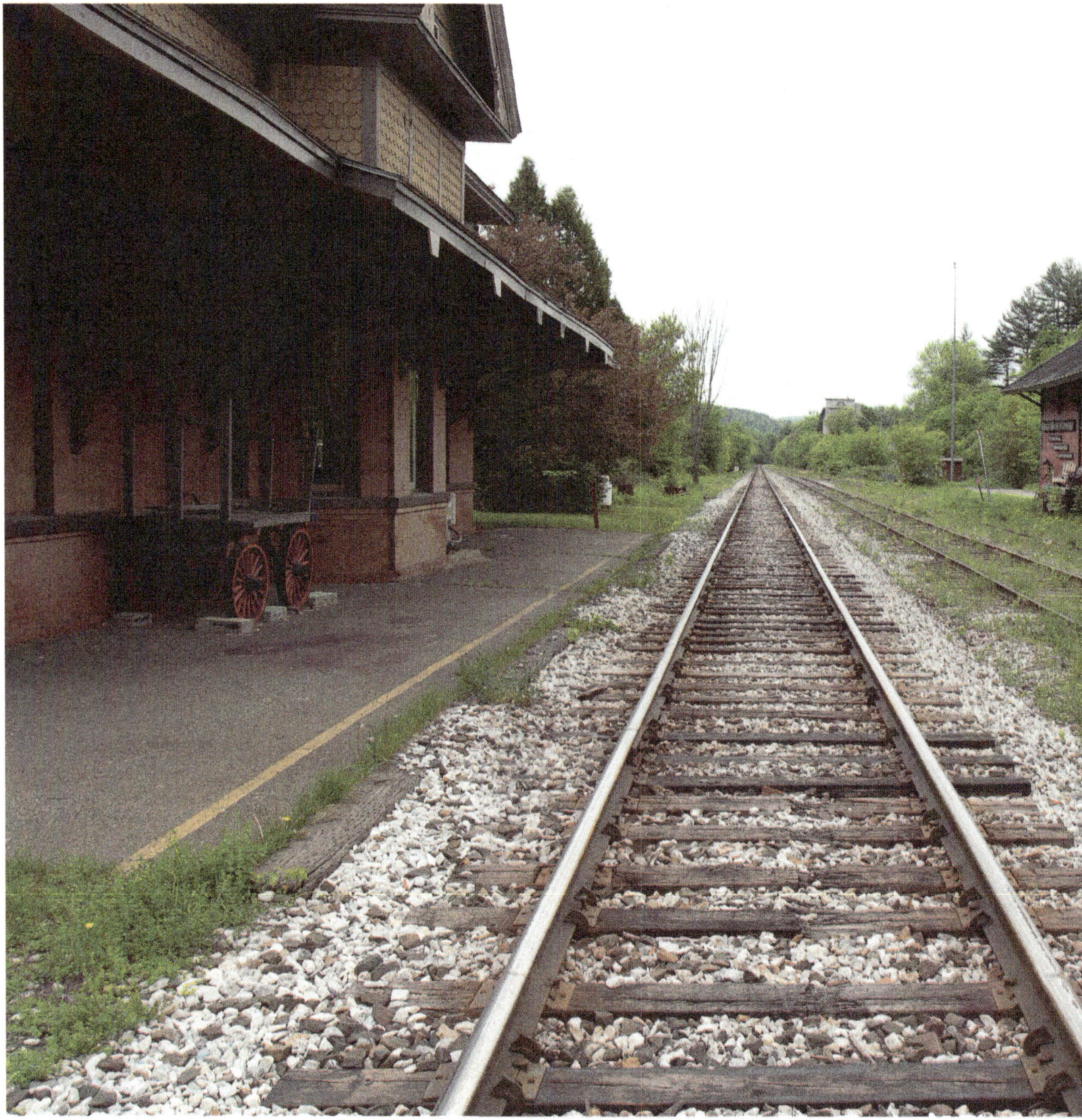

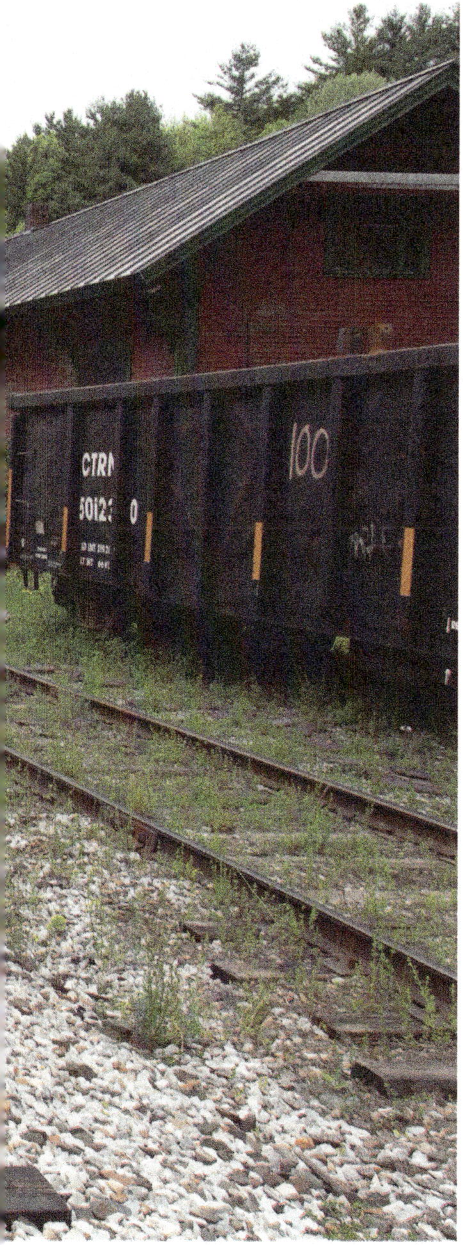

I-91, EXIT 20: PASSUMPSIC/ ST. JOHNSBURY (Route 5)

May 24, 9:00 a.m. Sun, morning mist

Easy grassy exit . . . but *Caution:*
Wires Overhead. Someone's
modernizing, stretching westward.
Cruise west toward Passumpsic
down winding Route 5 (where
Timothy Ide built Vermont's first
grist mill in 1819; it's gone). Miss it
in an eye-blink. Turn back, slow, and
park: yup, Passumpsic General Store
set back under a row of old maples,
Passumpsic Baptist Church tucked away
toward the railroad tracks and river.
Pumpkin yellow houses pop
behind purple lilacs, hedge trimmers
hum in the morning, and
the small falls of Passumpsic
River cascade into town. *Can I*
help you find something? asks a guy
in a pickup truck. *Nope, we're just*
visiting exit ramps and small Vermont
towns. We're in love with this one.
He beams: *Yup, a hidden gem*
on a May morning. Now you ask me
in mid-winter, when my heater's
on the blink, and the road's a
bear, and I'll give you another
answer . . . . Back under the caution

wires we go, east toward St. J.
This way follows the oldest industries:
railroad yard with a half-dozen tracks
and switch rails, concrete factories, broken
windows, old chimneys and silos.
Tempered Maple Corp. (*turned
many, many of our maple trees
into bowling pins*), Ralston Mill
(*former site of Purina Puppy Chow*),
E.T. & H.K. Ide Co. Plant (*oldest
company in Vermont, six generations
of millers bringing grain from the West
to Yankee farmers*), line the railroad
into town. From here, take the Main Street
bridge or the old railroad underpass:
Warning: Sound Horn—a caution
since 1899 when *the sign was erected
to avoid buggy collisions.* Today,
nobody takes the underpass unless
they want a collision with the past.

I-91, EXIT 21: ST. JOHNSBURY (Route 2, 15)
May 24, 10:00-11:00 a.m. Sun, clouds

The ramp's a swooping, timeless curve, make that
a horseshoe, a rainbow, a perfect parabolic arc,
like luck or justice that turns us north to south.
Cloverleaf so spacious it holds a full-blown marsh.

Swoop east to town, past St. Johnsbury Academy,
where public meets private: students with serious
resources and students without. In 1842 Thaddeus
Fairbanks weighed the scales of justice: for my sons

and all the town's children, "free moral, intellectual
and religious training." He was as good as his word
for thirty years. Made his fortune from scales
and weights, all balancing the balance sheets

so what was free was freely seen at the Fairbanks
Museum—zoological, ethnological, meteorological—
where today's Eye-on-the-Sky guys forecast the day's
downpours or shafts of sun from an airless,

soundproof room. Athenaeum's library & gallery
recall better days—Greek, Medieval—as seen
in the mind's eye, when Essence preceded Existence
and the undeserving deserved their fates.

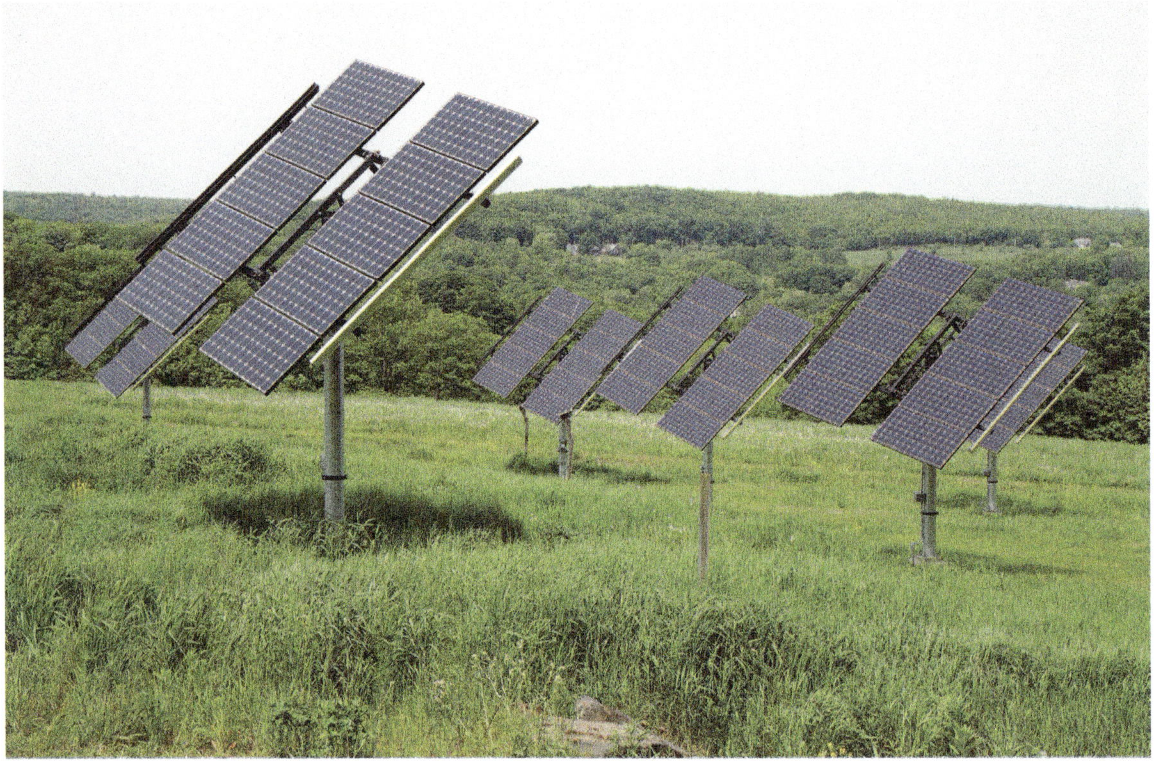

Eventually, the scales fall
from our eyes and we see the balance
mismeasured by partisan humans who cheered
the Greeks more than their slaves, or caved

to some convention that raised the rafters
of the Church higher than the heretics'.
In modern times, the Academy's mission
changed, embracing those they'd turned away,

darker brothers and sisters from the cities.
Then followed a golden age which raised the many,
for a while. Then, mills and factories failed. And many
suffered in a kind of new dark age. In northern

latitudes it's life jury-rigged, three jobs to a day's wage,
one job in the woods, one in town, and long waits
for federal aid to make the balance balance.
Fairbanks Scales never failed. 1400 workers

still toil in the factories, but the smart execs
and marketers moved to Kansas City, maybe
a few Academy grads among them, if justice
is just. For those with other aptitudes,

there are heating and cooking stoves to repair
(Fairbanks invented 'em), cast iron plows
to grind and weld (Fairbanks invented 'em),
hemp to grow (Fairbanks grew it long ago!).

After work, leisure: Catamount Arts for theater,
stargazing at the Fairbanks Planetarium,
and lofty paintings of the Hudson River school
lit from skylights of the Athenaeum.

All in a day's—a decade's, a century's—work,
Thaddeus might have said, this man whose scales
weighed the heavy loads of the world,
from London to Beijing, Tokyo to San Francisco,

and judged invention, a good patent, a means
of production, and lastly, leisure, to be the essence
of what passes for living in these northern towns
founded on a balanced, human scale.

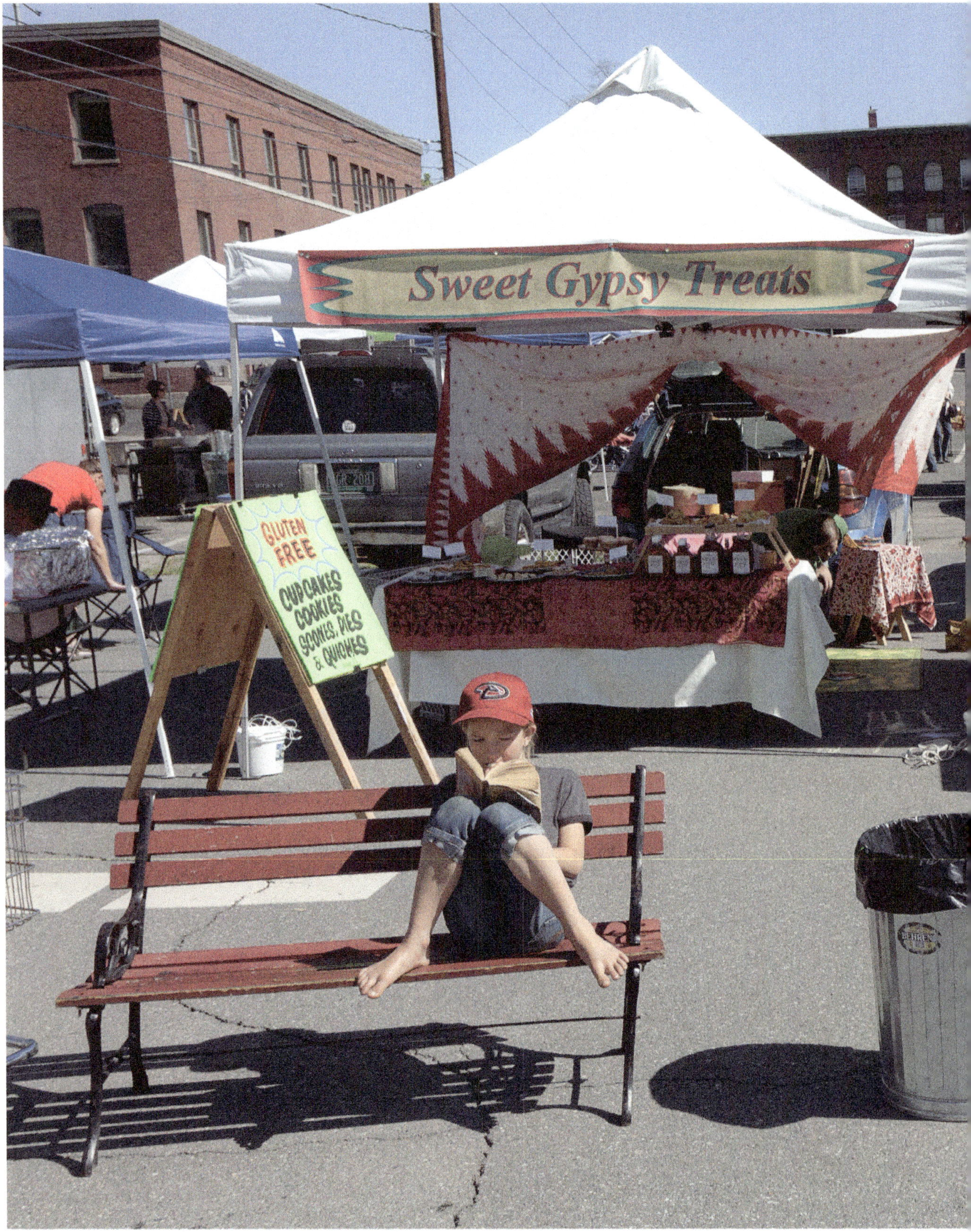
Sweet Gypsy Treats
GLUTEN FREE
CUPCAKES
COOKIES
SCONES, PIES
& QUICHES

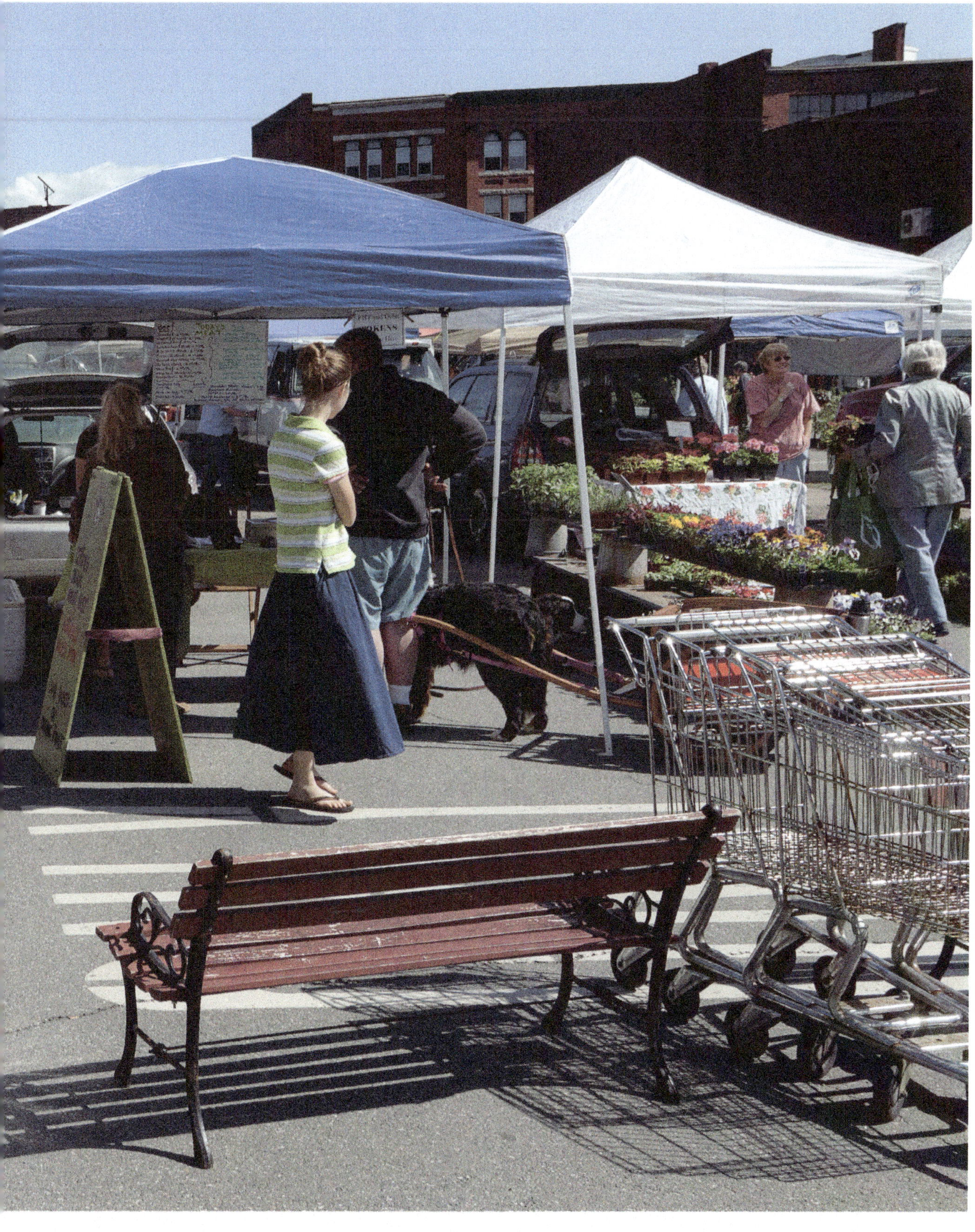

I-91, EXIT 22: ST. JOHNSBURY (Route 5)
May 24, noon-time. Sun, clouds

Start at a point
where your foot lifts off the gas,
you slow down a long, gaunt ramp,
and meet the feeder road to Route 5.

Let us consider the feeder road
and what it feeds. A lunch-time line
of motorists considers it with you, stalled
at a light where the truck route nears the market.

The feeding begins on a strip
north of town, where Price Chopper
competes with KFC & Taco Bell & Pizza Hut.
Farther on, you could stop for a quick one (with strips

of beef jerky) at the Gold Eagle
Lanes or drink deeply at the Black Bear
Tavern or end at the Elks Club for old covers—
"Ain't Gonna Eat Out My Heart Anymore" (The
Rascals)

and "Boom Boom Boom Boom" (The Animals)
dished up on a Saturday with hot dogs and beer.

Thaddeus Fairbanks,
what think ye? Have we met
your highest requirements? Is the diet
sufficient? Would you have feasted or starved,

balancing your scales?
Granted, we're far from the old agora,
town center. We're relegated to the cross-
roads, the unruly edge, one foot into the wilderness.

Nevertheless, would you
have shaped this place for civic
purpose—park or playground—or would you
have left it thus, transient culture at the edge of empire

from Ebla to Petra, Doura to Palmyra,
a place of passage, sustenance wolfed and quaffed
by travelers coming or going along the trade routes, locals
or strangers, from Antioch to Athens, Seleucia to Carthage?

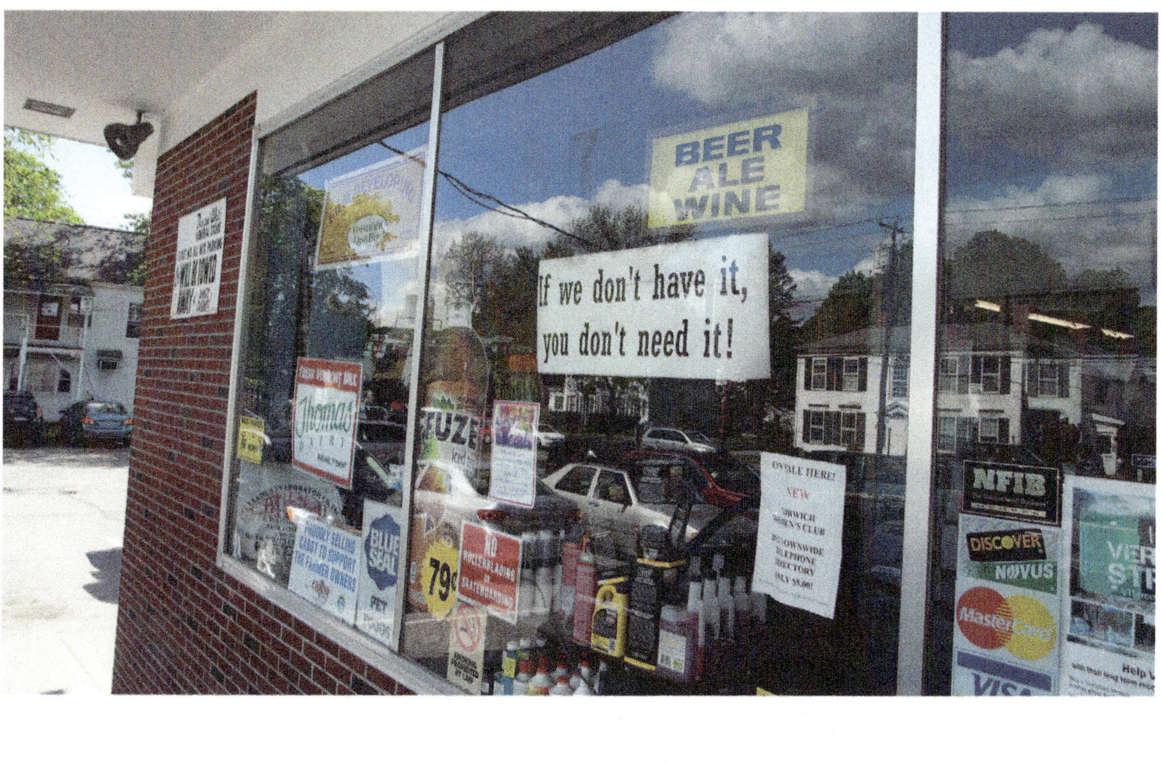

I-91, EXIT 23: LYNDONVILLE (Routes 5, 14)

May 24, 12:30-1:30 p.m. Sun, clouds
"Lyndon State College ahead"

Decline along a triangle of land; the engine
backfires, belches, stalls. The pines
are pretty, smell pitchy. Route 5's alive

with chains: Dunkin Ds, McDs, Domino's.
And one unchained: Pizza Man! Faster
than an airborne pie dervishing off his thumb,

more powerful than an army of delivery boys
(*his* orders are internetted "quick pick-up"),
able to rent one building without bouncing

a check (!) he outcompetes "the mind-forged
manacles" of strips. Ask a Lyndon girl
if there's a decent place to eat in town,

she'll say, "Pizza Man, but he's just pick-up.
Sorry, there's nary a restaurant." (Her grandma
said it, too.) Perhaps she's scared of outsiders,

scared to surrender the secret: Carmen's,
farm-to-table gem, ice cream stand & cafe.
My, my, my ~ 60 flavors later, your belly's heavy.

Home-made corn & lobster chowder, chipotle
vegetable sandwich on sourdough, fresh-baked
apple crumble with a few scoops of cinnamon-

vanilla do you in. Tomorrow's graduation on the hill,
some sententious speaker paid way too much
to deliver the measure of a senior—something

about "service" and "real world" and "service
industry." Today the town's deserted so let's chill
and add a little depth (and girth) to character.

Then walk a block to the perpetually failing Green
Mountain Books, full of books, empty of patrons,
and see if there's a book on spirituality

that's literate, emptied of platitudes, empty
in exactly the right soul-building way—
love of the One and the many, and each

creature with a direct, original relation to Creation.

That's how you arrive at 60 unequaled creamy confections.
That's how the Girl Who Says Nary will, finally, tarry
with a boy from "away" and hold him close, anyway.

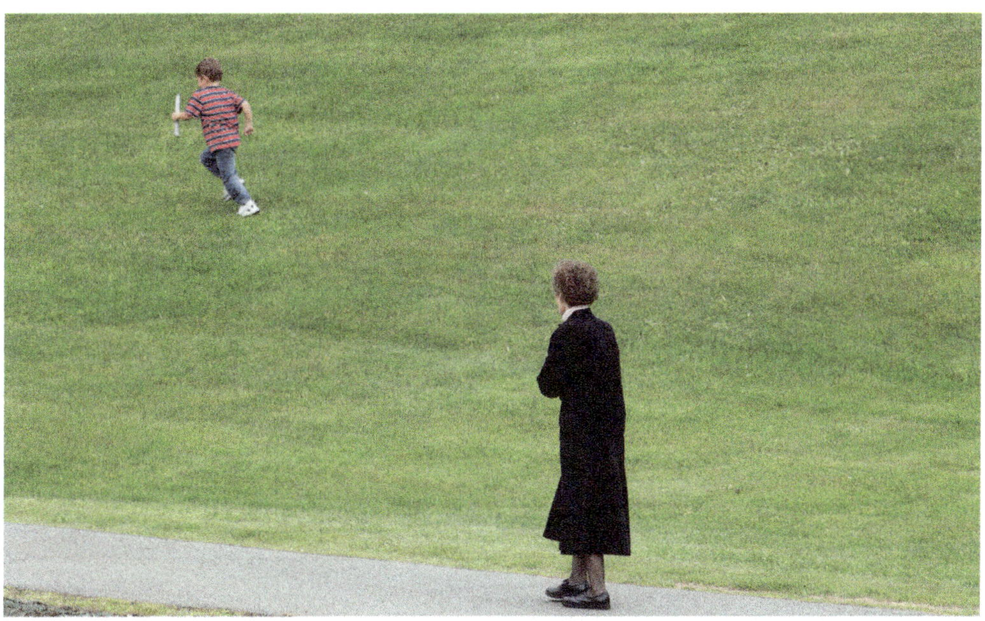

I-91, EXIT 24: WHEELOCK (Route 122)

May 24, Sun, clouds

Huge expanse as the state ascends to its unpopulated north—
exit ramps wind through hillsides, through microzones I can imagine
in my secret mind. *Alpaca Farm Days* posts the only sign to help my
conjuring. I don a wool sweater and drive five miles to a Wheelock
I conceive rising along Gilman Rd, along the rushing Passumpsic.
Feeder brooks—Fall, Squabble, Mathewson—plush with water,
feed the pools and eddying currents deeper than memory,
rush and rise up to Peak Road and Vertical Mile, where views
spill over watersheds shedding waters west to Sheffield and over
the long course to the county-coursing Lamoille, east to the state-
splitting Connecticut. Sulfur springs make a stink in the town's
memory—used to be medicinal. Now the stink is mostly cow shit,
hillside farms rank with it. Wheelock's the only town composed
and chartered from beyond. New Hampshire owns it.
Chartered by Dartmouth, from its founder, Eleazar Wheelock,
to his son (the College's first president), John Wheelock.
Yep, the wheels have a lock on this pavement, but the land
belongs to farmers with other names: Reid, Ramsey, Sawyer.
And the day-school belongs to Sheffield. The cemetery to Dexter.
The whole of it belongs to my mind bubbling and roiling with the
state's tributaries, ramps and roadways and rivers to get me there,
even when I'm a Google-Earth map away, a twin river, the Seine,
out my window, with willows and poplars blowing in a steady rain.
James Joyce had his Dublin map and phonebook while he sat in

Paris or Trieste. From Dante to Conrad, the great expatriates
mapped out their beloved abandoned cities. Does it matter
what exile moves the mind's currents and sends them coursing
over places half-remembered, half-invented? These constitute
our allegiances and affections, the mysterious GPS of our inner
nature, navigating a landscape that will not let us drift or waver.
I have run every year for the town's select-board. I oversee
the road-crews, mow the cemetery lawns, dispatch
the feral dogs, and wade into the wide Passumpsic to save
the drowning child. I am the town's secret hope, honored
each day at the Post Office with the raising of the flag,
the lowering of the lift at Cole's Automotive, my thumbprint
on the town's approval of septic plans and setbacks,
foundation sites and concrete slabs (annually awarded to Bob's
Construction, with 30 years' experience on the ground), while
I supervise with 60 years of experience from a bird's-eye view,
hieratic, gyroscopic, floating over, positioned and pinpointed—
the mind's eye that relays images from a satellite in inner space.
I co-sign attestations with Carol Rossi: the delinquent taxes
have been paid. I attend to the myriad complaints of the residents:
the potholes will be filled, the leaky roof of the church patched,
and soon the internet service will improve. I am beaming down
this poem from far off, bouncing it off satellites in hopes that one day
soon they will have the capacity and connectivity to read it.

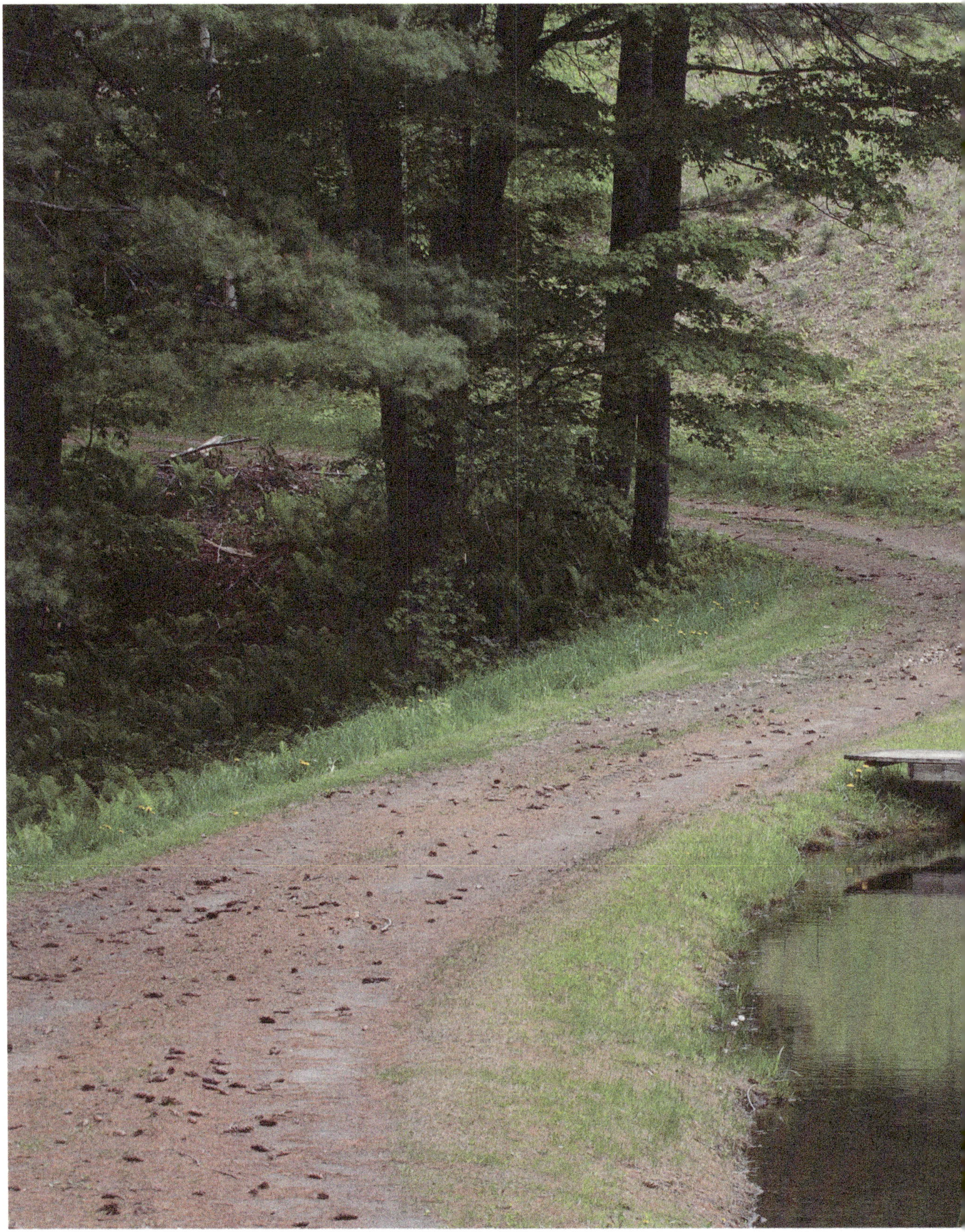

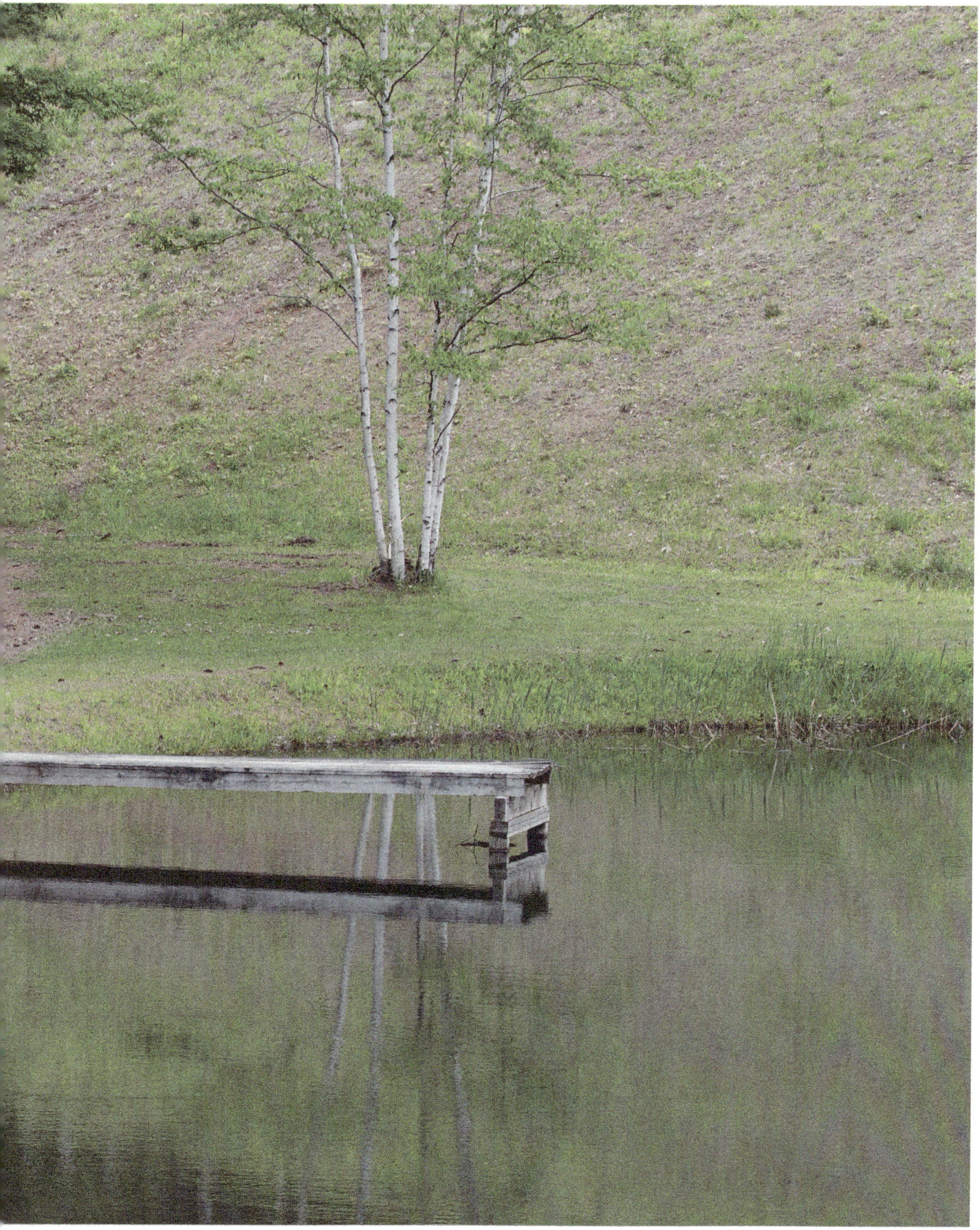

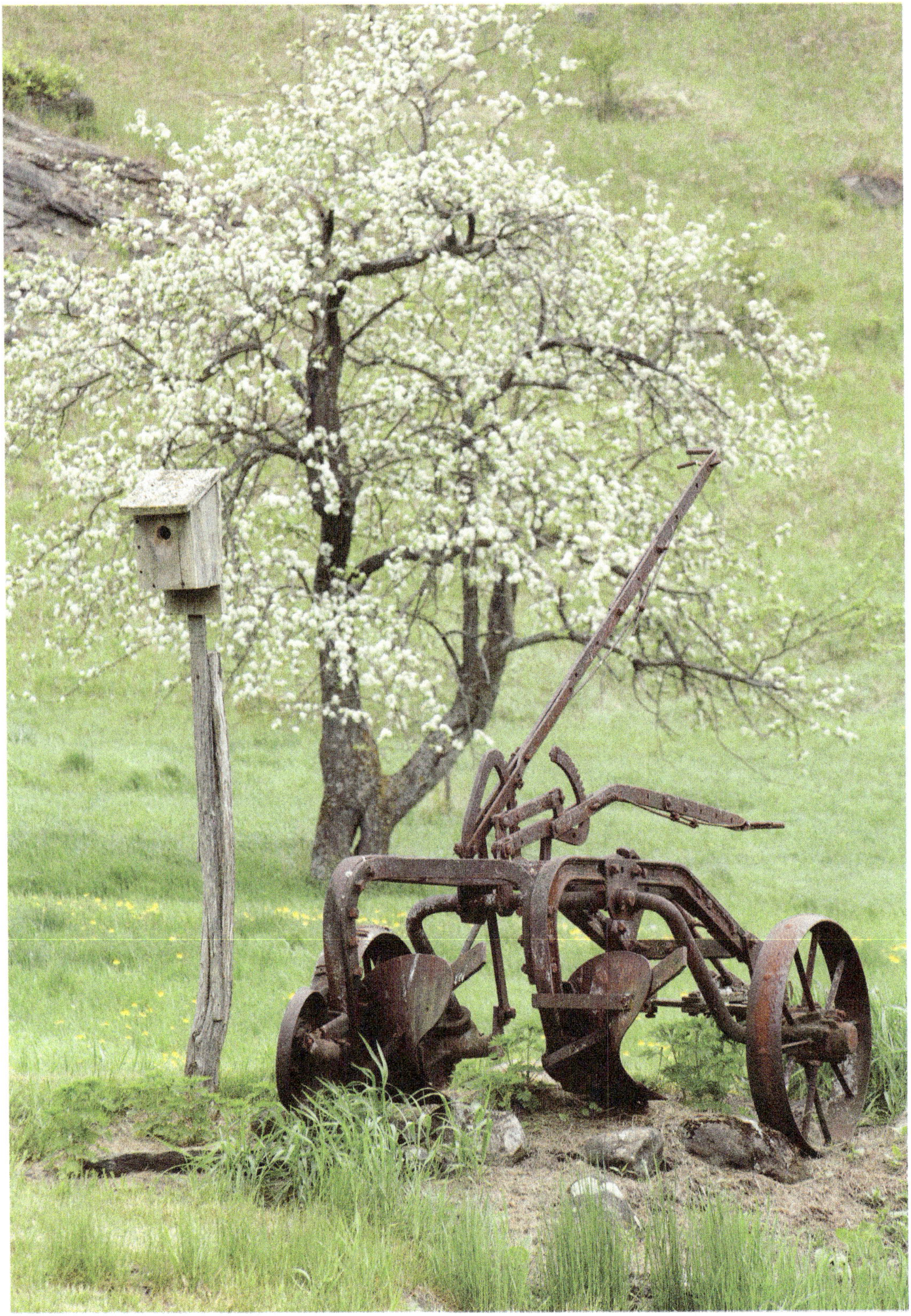

I-91, EXIT 25: BARTON/GLOVER (Route 16 to 5)

May 24, 1:45-2:30 p.m. Sun, clouds

Before Barton, highway's highest elevation:
1856 feet at Mile Marker 150.4: Olympian
air: then the long decline to valley towns:

Barton, down a long ramp, crab apples
claiming a triangle of dandelion pasture.
Farm silos straight ahead, barns,

tire piles, dairy cows, chickens, the real
deal. Solid Rock Church Assembly of God
husbands souls, leaves the rest to farms.

Downtown is down: stores boarded up,
scrum of men bear-hugging and guzzling
beer on the street, old couples gazing

from sagging porches. Nearby, Most Holy
Trinity (1902) needs to fill its church
coffers for a paint job. *Your Hydraulic*

Hose Headquarters is the most
alliterative firm in town. Next door, Win-
nebagos on wheels, trailers on

concrete blocks. And Roaring Brook
runs through it, ready to rise
if God's mind turns to rain.

Glover is richer. Still, more Rockwell
than Rockefeller. Picture this: two enormous
workhorses hitched to a skidder. On the carriage

seat grandfather, father, son, sitting
at the intersection of Still Hill Road
and Main Street, at the intersection of

yesterday and today. At first, it seems
they're giving horse-rides . . . or giving
horses a rest from hauling logs . . .

But no . . . there's no load . . . they're just
watching traffic, posing as pastoral
anachronisms on Saturday afternoon

in the year of someone's lord, 2013,
and someone else's 4711, or 5773,
until all of time is accounted for

and human leisure is accounted for
on Still Hill Road, so
named, no doubt, for stills

that brewed another leisure here.
Long gone. Now, the general store
provides. As does Busy Bee Diner,

a half-trailer serving burgers and fries.
A few miles farther, there's another Glover,
Bread and Puppet Theater, overseer

of present spectacle and past wonder,
of old miracles and new crimes against us all
from far, far afield, enacted here in an earthen

amphitheater the envy of Ephesus so that time
is a construct that avails not, space is
a construct that avails not, we see

eye to eye how the world abides
its miseries and we cannot hide
in a deep declivity, no, not here.

I-91, EXIT 26: ORLEANS (Route 5, 58)

May 24, 3:00-4:00 pm. Sun, clouds

"Exit for Irasburg, Lake Willoughby"

The ramp's ho-hum. Time for a time-
out: at this hour in Orleans,
France, they're sipping apéritifs
along the Loire, evaluating what they owe
to Julius Caesar (hail Caesar,
not a passing waiter) whose Roman
Aurelian shares its name (Orleans), how
Charlemagne brought them enlightenment,
how Joan of Arc wrested the city from the Brits
and gave it back to France.
Vive la France!

Stop dreaming. Here, let's hope Ethan Allen
Furniture Assembly Manufacturing Center
is a coup for the 800 residents and not a coup
de grâce. Let's hope it still employs
400 workers on its 85 acres of factories,
that there's good ventilation and benefits
the envy of farmers and pharmacists
throughout the county! Not a café table,
not a *gouté* hour, not a *clochard*
or *flaneur* in sight . . . unfair to ask, perhaps,
of a factory town or a farming community . . .
maybe a happy hour, an espresso bar . . .

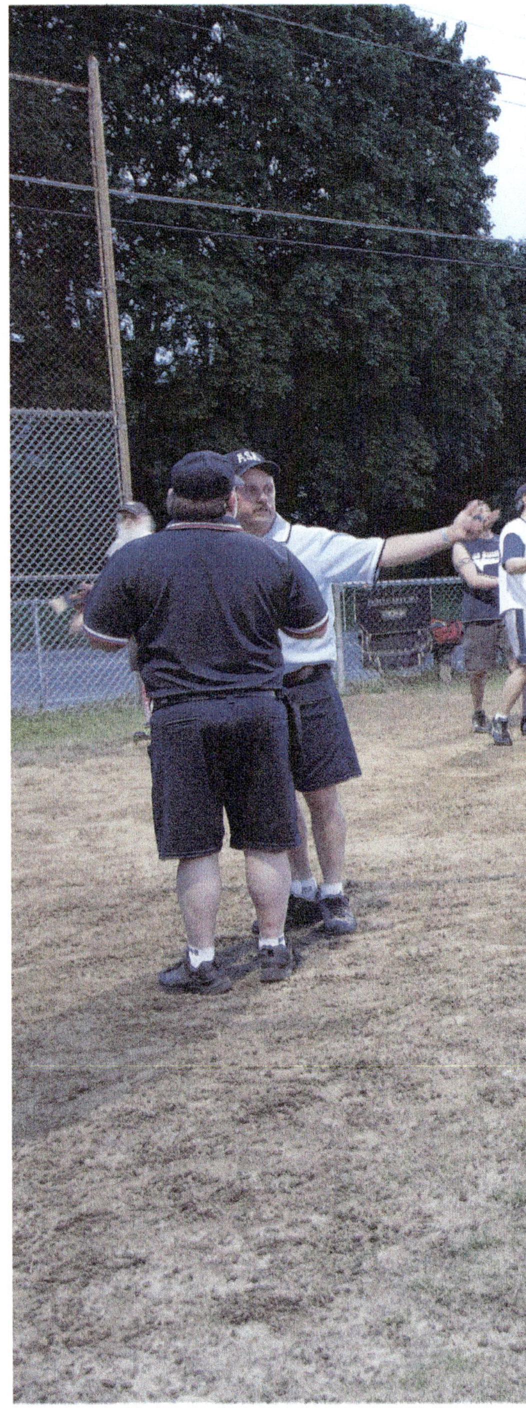

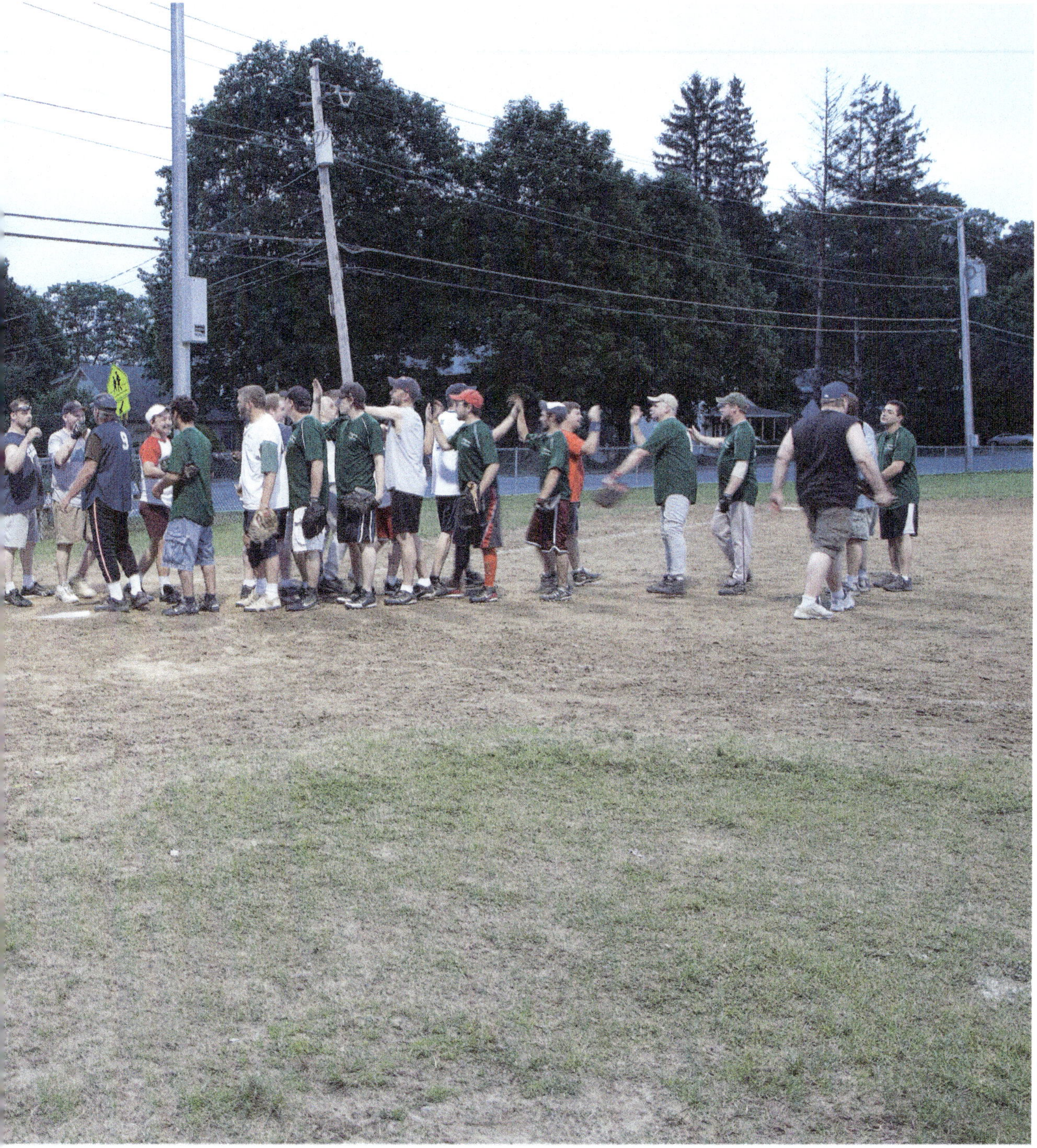

Stop dreaming! Drive east to Willoughby, deepest
lake in the state, so deep a drowned man's body
vanished, washed up weeks later in another lake,
swooped through subterranean caverns so un-
conscious there are creatures we've never seen . . .
Stop dreaming! Drive west toward Irasburg,
the Lowell range in the distance with wind
turbines NIMBYing the peaks, humming
megawatts and transforming the air . . .

Stop dreaming! Orleans is so unseen *The Kingdom*
Guide ("guiding tourists to attractions
in the Northeast Kingdom") doesn't see it.
If they did, they'd bless its secret name:
Barton Landing. They'd tally how many
of its sons perished in the Civil War.
They'd calculate the French Canadians
who descended to purchase the dead
ones' farms. Barton Landing buried
a lot of bodies. Then changed
its name: Orleans. At the edge
of the village, Willoughby Falls,
200 foot stretch of water with cascades
and chutes. These days, trout migrate
up the falls and spawn where they recall
Barton Landing . . . Stop dreaming!

In Orleans, when they dream
of culture, they mean the town
library, or Catholic prayer, or the *frisson*
of one formal dance, the *galop*.
Folks like to speculate on Gerald Bull
and his supersonic weapons they'd hear
near the border. Killed in Brussels,
they say, assassinated by somebody
who didn't want a weapon in their
backyard. Brussels . . . that's a long way
away . . . café tables aplenty, French
speakers sipping apéritifs and Leffe beers,
talking sex and metaphysics . . . Stop dreaming!

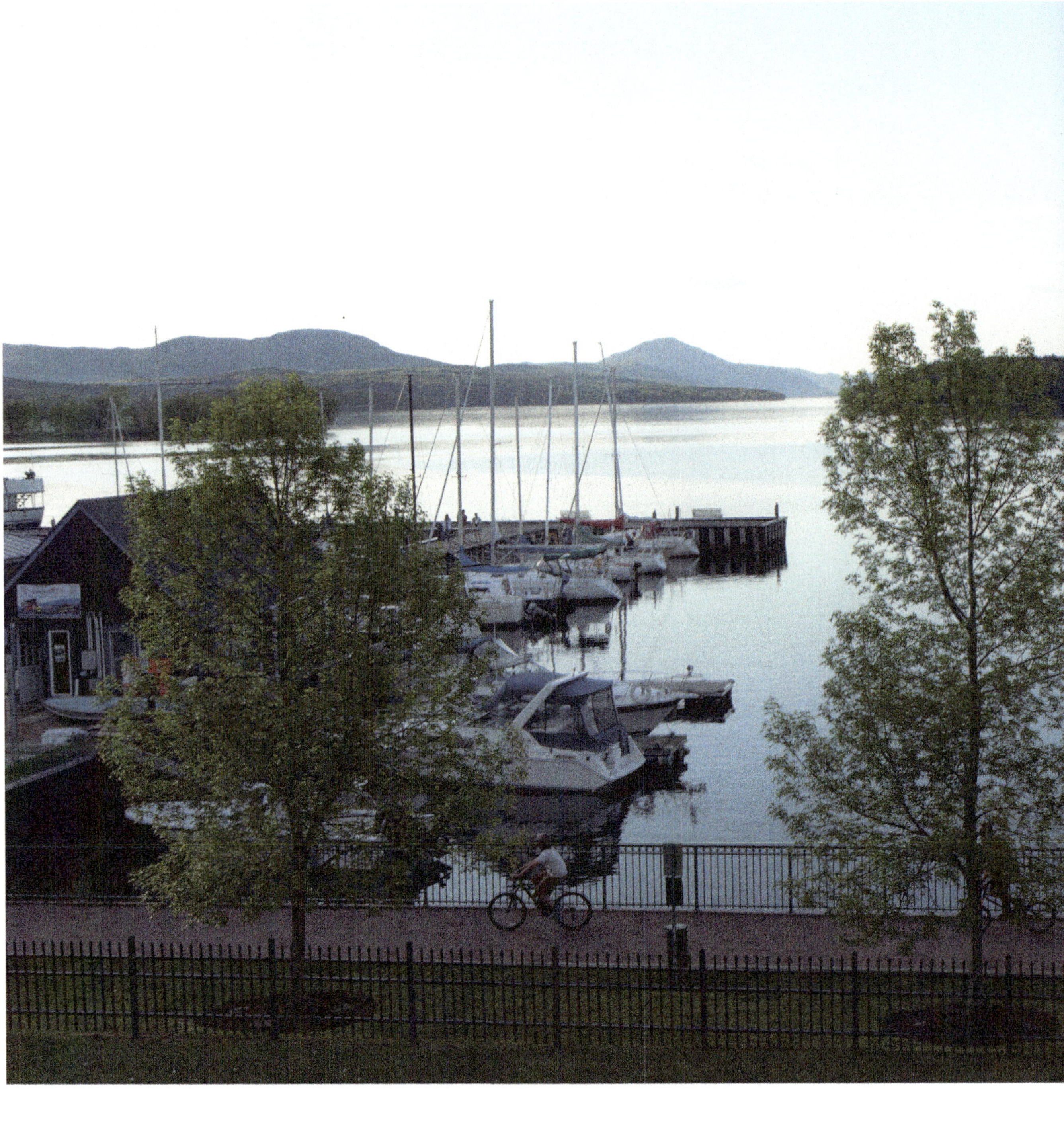

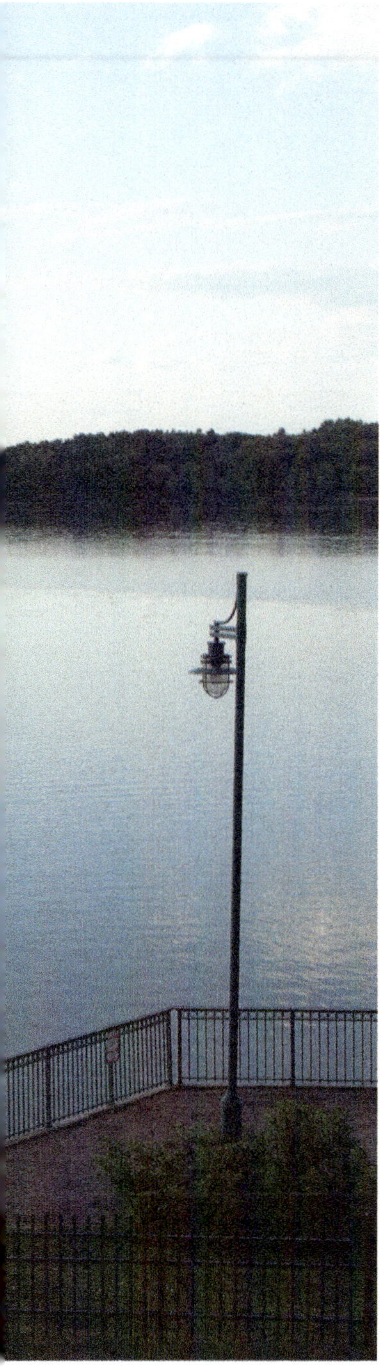

I-91, EXIT 27: NEWPORT (Routes 5, 105, 191)
May 24, 4:00-5:00 p.m. Full sun

Circle exit—full 360—with granite flanks.
Pine forest, pitched thick and cryptic.
Then the two-mile plunge to Newport

where the Memphremagog refreshes us,
our eyes agog with luminous surprise,
miles and miles of open water across

the northern border into Canada.
Coast Guard cruises an imaginary line.
The drugs they confiscate are real.

As they say in the vernacular: good shit.
Motto: Seize it and none will come.
So Newport has had to renew itself:

former Abenaki fishing ground,
former lumber town, former steam-
boat stop, former livery stable,

former railroad stop, former
Teddy Bear maker, former forest-products
maker, former ski-wear maker, now—

gentrified city of services, the waterfront
a waterfront worth walking, now
sailboats in the bay, restaurants

on shore. The lake's an open
eye whose sky is perfectly starry
when the weather's friendly.

O it can be temperamental in autumn,
full of bluster and chop, and it can frost
your ass in winter, and in summer

it can turn so hazy and forgetful it hardly says
hello... But in May, today, sun in blue sky,
it's perfectly alert, a mirror near shore, and farther out

it's glinting and spirited and pulls the hills
right down to it. All that new green and gold
spills right into the ridges of the waves.

So one must really make an effort to turn
and study the muddy imperfections
of the town, the rusted train-tracks, the rutted roads,

the aging Russian Orthodox Church gloomy
over the town. In mind's eye, I still see
the run-down bars and haggard players

in the pool halls, garage-band musicians
trying to keep it real while they await
the next shipment of ganja or hash.

The Chinese take-out always changing
windows, shattered from rocks or fists.
Abenakis arrested for no reason, Owl's Head

peak looming in the western sky. Now, turn
back to the lake and see sailboats dazzling
the water. See how they make a *port new*.

One chance *per town* to turn it around.

I-91, EXIT 28: DERBY CENTER (Routes 5, 111, 105)
May 24, 5:30-6:30 p.m. Sun, clouds

Short exit with nothing on it.
Almost nothing: a butchered bush.
A sign: *Cow Palace Steak & Lounge.*

At the intersection of 5 & 111, there it is:
sprawling restaurant with an antler
arch for an entrance. We're talking antlers,

hundreds hacked off and stacked together
until they form a kind of bleached
rainbow under which God's

covenant with man fronts on blood.
An acre's car-lot opens onto pasture
where elk herds wait for slaughter.

While dining at the Cow Palace,
please take a moment to enjoy
one of America's most regal animals,

the Elk, who make the land
adjoining our restaurant their home.
Don't say I'm an antler-hugger;

I'm a carnivore, but when I picture
the live rack skimming treeline
faster than the brush of an eyelash,

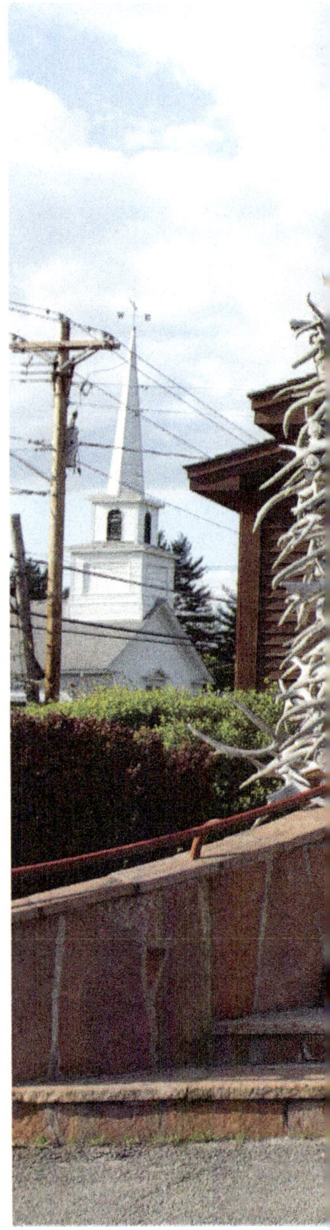

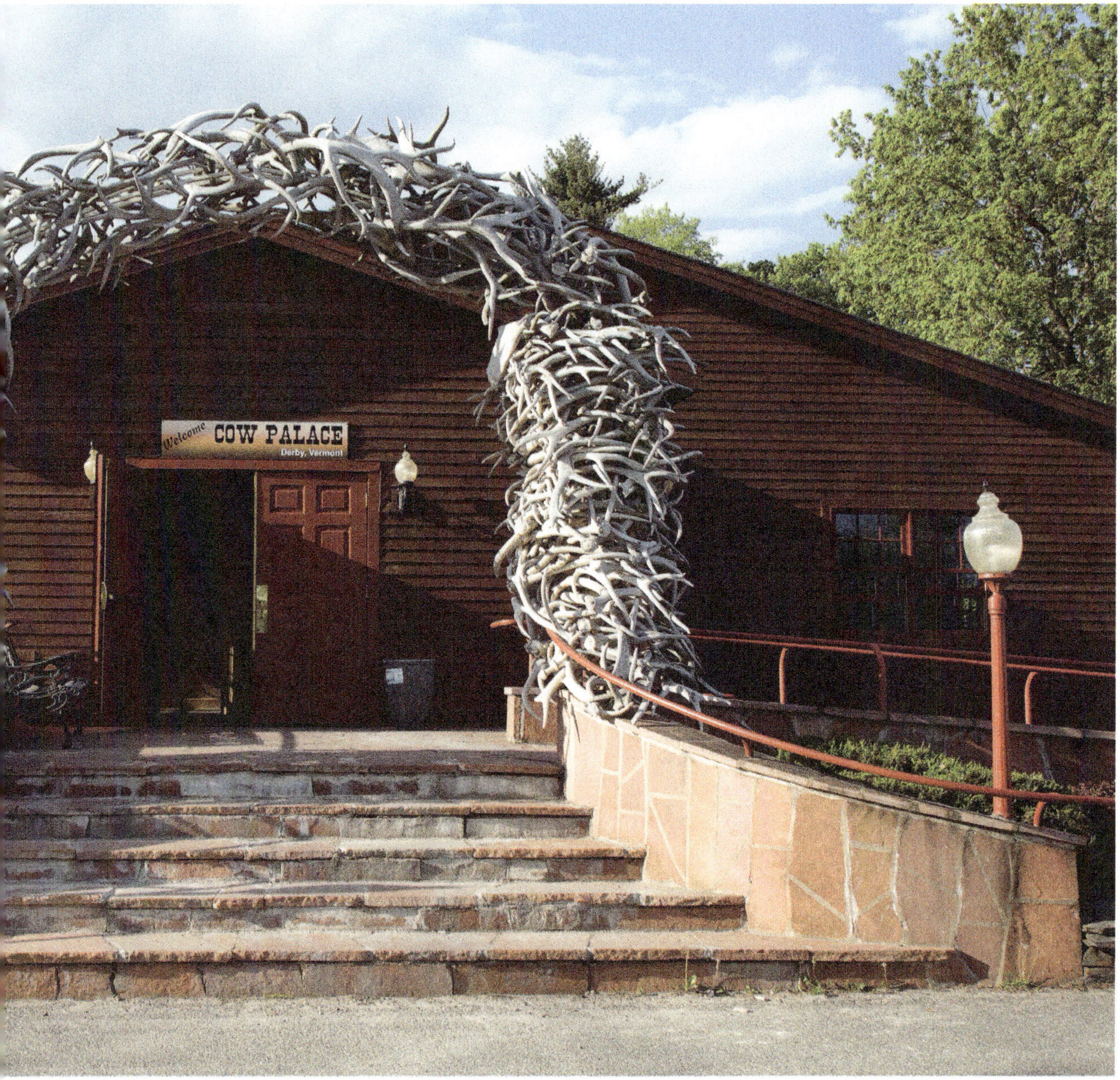
Welcome COW PALACE
Derby, Vermont

this bloodless bull elk architecture turns
my stomach, turns me to a ruminant
ruminating on sacrifice. Otherwise,

the town is nice. Soaring church
next door. Stately houses reminiscent of
privilege everywhere, long lawns opening

on alpine meadows that overlook (the Elk) the
distant Whites. Lake Salem winks nearby.
Lake Seymour winces in the distance.

Old shade trees overhead, old elms
survived the blight that killed kin
less north than this. For some

things, then, this north is life
and not the blighted sacrifice.
This is a peaceful town with State Police.

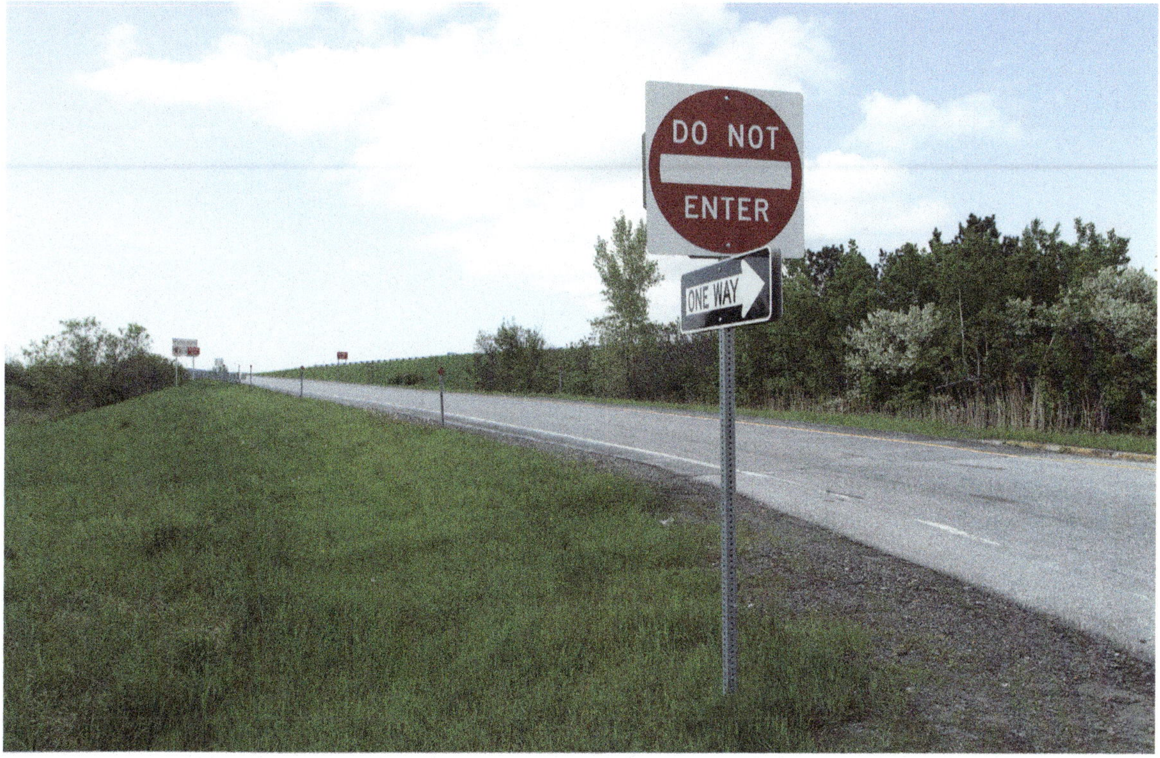

I-91, EXIT 29: DERBY LINE (Route 5)

May 24, 6:30-7:30 p.m. Sun, clouds, sunset
"Border Ahead"/45 N Latitude/Mile Marker 176

Exhaustion and surrender: too many hours on the road,
too many dreams deferred. "US Customs/Immigration Ahead."
Whatever we carried in our minds, the photos, the poems,
is a weight, a freight we surrender at the sunset border.
"All Overseas Cargo Stops Here for Inspection." What
can we carry with us beyond the sea where memory
lapses? Nothing that we know. Apparently, we leave it
here, at the border, between one state and another.
Last exit barely offers a farewell, a few perfunctory
trees, a few patches of grass. Last exit barely hides
its contempt for the traveler's besotted state,

ready for long sleep, a dream in which
death and taxes are deferred until the ending
of the afterworld. Fat chance. Your best bet
is to get a library card from Haskell Free
Library in Derby Line, enter the front door
in America, exit the back door in Canada
(with *Vermont Exit Ramps* in your satchel),
and hope the eternal Border Patrol's snoozing
behind the tinted-glass security van. The vanity
of borders! As if divinity promised us.
Upstairs, the opera house is in crisis,
one melodrama, and another, when
the truth they sought was simply love.
But humans have a way of bellowing and
wailing when they should be whispering.
We still don't understand the passion in
a passion play is for mortal stakes and
has more to do with agapé than agony . . .
Or is it just the other way? Suffering, as always.
Black line down the middle of the check-out room
marks the border you cannot cross without
crossing toward your arrest and true conviction.

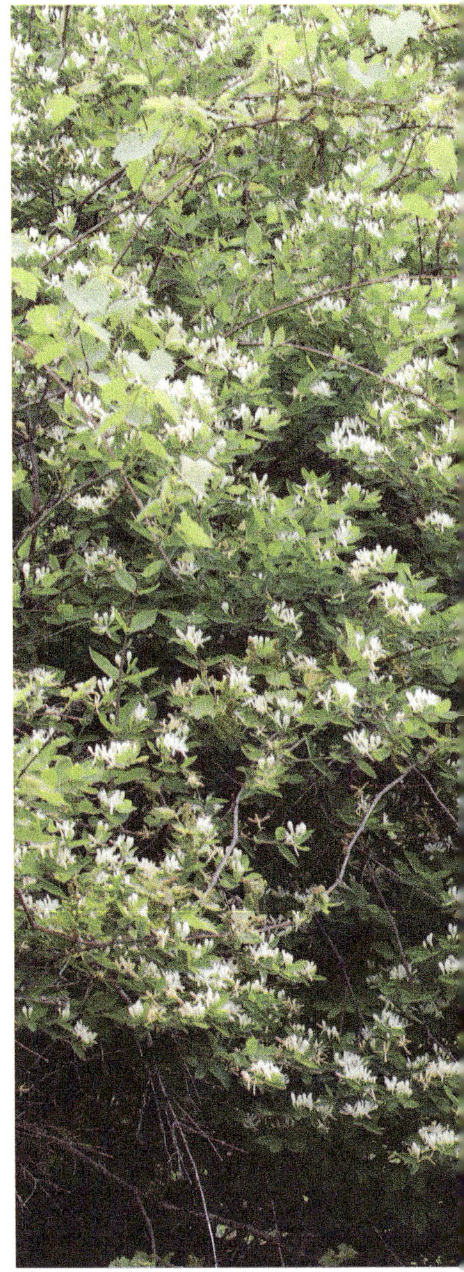

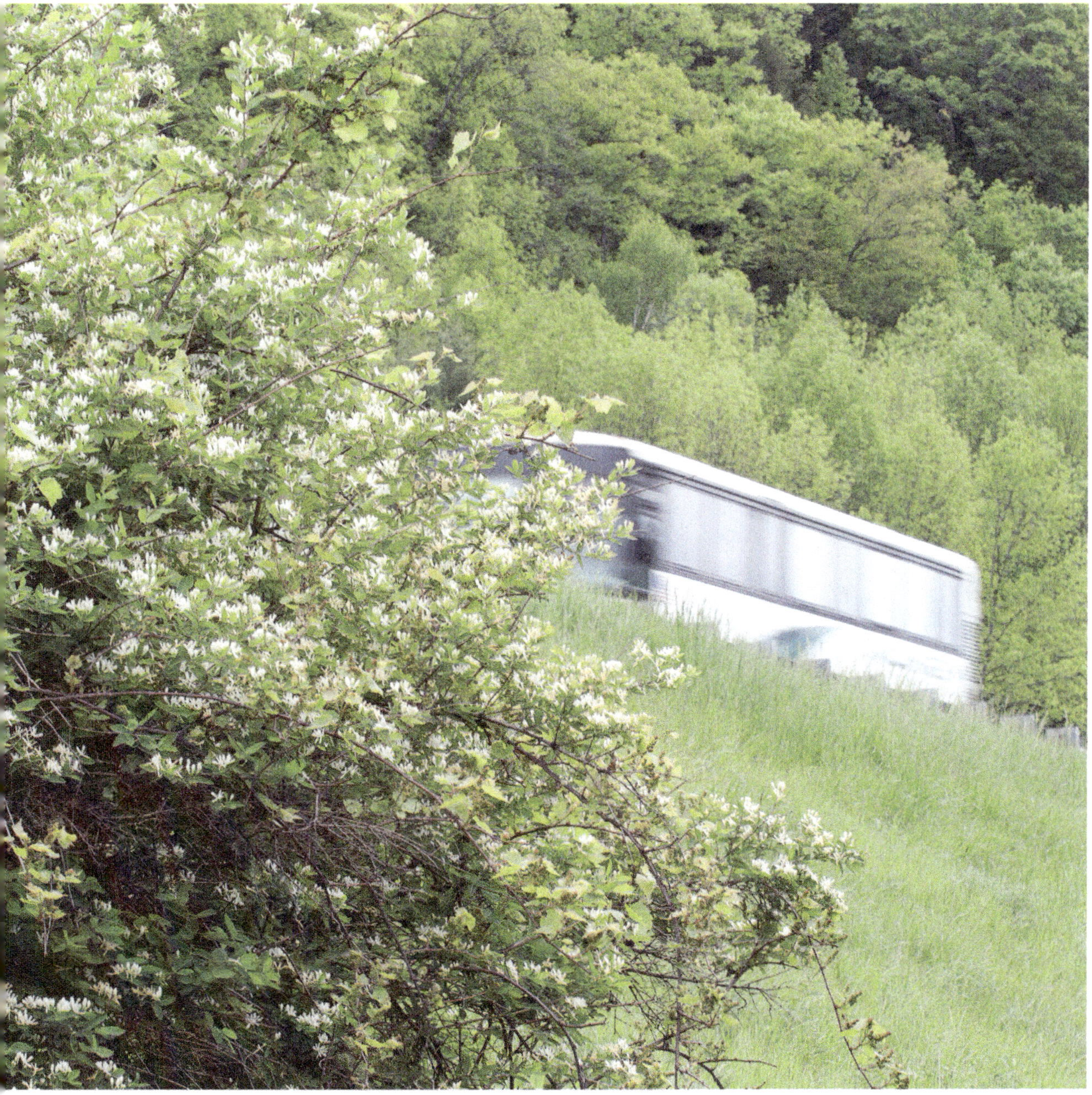

Acknowledgments

In addition to those I acknowledged in the final paragraph of my Introduction (p. xiii), let me also thank Terese Svoboda, Tony Whedon, and Jay White, all of whom made invaluable suggestions for the improvement of *Vermont Exit Ramps II*. Let me thank, as well, *Hunger Mountain Review*, where the following poems first appeared in print: "I-89, Exit 6: South Barre," "I-89, Exit 10: Stowe/Waterbury," "I-89, Exit 17: Colchester/Champlain Islands," "I-89, Exit 18: Fairfax/Georgia." Finally, let me thank Ramola D, editor of *Delphi Quarterly*, whose interview with me about the original chapbook, *Vermont Exit Ramps*, was excerpted and transformed into *Vermont Exit Ramp II*'s "Introductory Interview with 8 Exit Ramps."

NS

When Neil called to invite me and my camera along on his *VER* journey, it was an easy decision to make. I would get the chance to both reconnect with an old college friend on a multi-day road trip, and wander around (and photograph) my home state of Vermont as Spring unfolded. I am grateful for that offer, and what has ensued.

It goes without saying that a project of this scope required the skills of many hands and hearts. Thanks especially to Tamra and Dede for all their work in bringing this book into print.

I would be much less a photographer (and person) without my sweetheart of nearly 30 years, my wife Celia. These are gifts I can, perhaps, never repay.

AR
September 2015

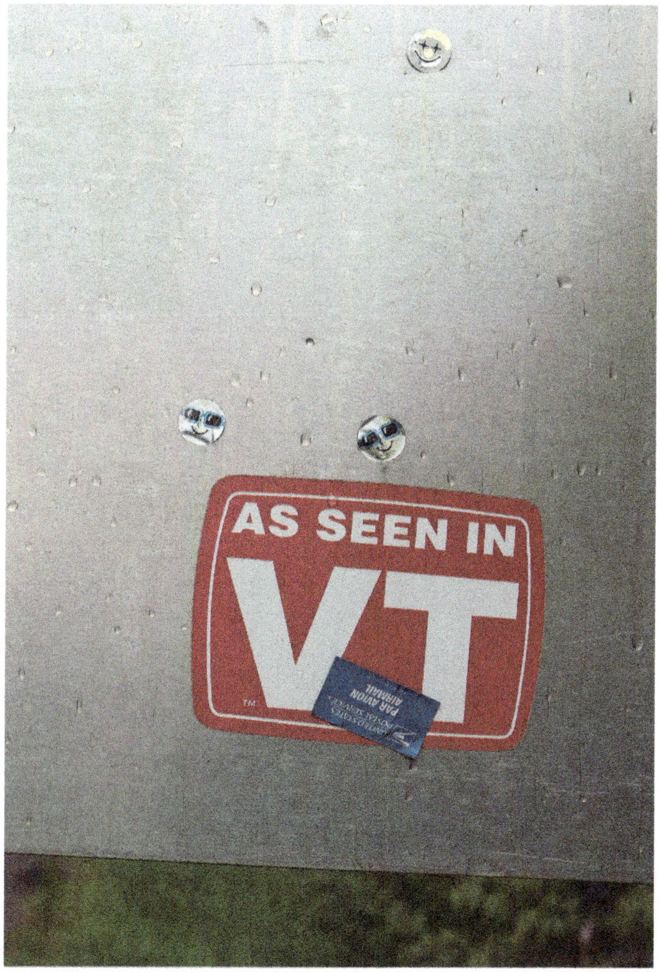
AS SEEN IN
VT

CPSIA information can be obtained at www.ICGtesting.com
Printed in the USA
LVOW05s1739191015

458881LV00002B/2/P

9 780996 267649